DAVID POWLISON

POWER ENCOUNTERS

Reclaiming Spiritual Warfare

HOURGLASS BOOKS

Baker Books

A Division of Baker Book House Co
Grand Rapids, Michigan 49516

Scripture quotations taken from the *Holy Bible, New International Version.* Copyright © 1973, 1978, 1984 by International Bible Society.

ISBN: 0-8010-7138-0

Seventh printing, February 2003

Printed in the United States of America

For current information about all releases from Baker Book House, visit our web site:

http://www.bakerbooks.com/

POWER
ENCOUNTERS

Hourglass Books are for all who long for reformation and revival within the evangelical community. As "tracts for the times" they raise major issues of the day. Each book is serious in tone and probing in style but practical rather than academic, more often a first word than the last. Designed not only to be read but discussed and acted on, Hourglass Books are for all who seek to restore the gospel to evangelicals and evangelicals to the gospel.

Books in the series:

- *Dining with the Devil: The Megachurch Movement Flirts with Modernity* by Os Guinness
- *The Evangelical Forfeit: Can We Recover?* by John Seel
- *Restoring the Good Society: A New Vision for Politics and Culture* by Don E. Eberly
- *Fit Bodies, Fat Minds: Why Evangelicals Don't Think and What to Do About It* by Os Guinness
- *Winning Words: A Call to Christian Persuasion* by William Edgar (forthcoming)
- *Haunted Houses: Ghostwriting and Religious Publishing* by Edward E. Plowman (forthcoming)

To Nan
a woman of valor and faith
in spiritual warfare.

CONTENTS

1 Reclaiming Spiritual Warfare   11

2 What Is Spiritual Warfare?   27

3 Ask Questions of the Text in Context   39

4 Cultures Dark with the Occult   49

5 Sin and Suffering   63

6 Jesus' Mode of Ministry and Ours   77

7 A Host of Further Questions   93

8 "Resist the Devil"   107

9 Rethinking the Details   121

10 A Better Way   137

   Notes   153

ACKNOWLEDGMENTS

My heartiest thanks:

To my colleagues at the Christian Counseling & Educational Foundation for providing time and opportunity to study, teach, and write on this subject;

To Amy Boucher and Os Guinness for outstanding work to improve the clarity of my writing;

To Vern Poythress and Alan Groves for their thoughtful reflections on Scripture and on their own experience;

To Warren Groves for the generosity and care with which he communicated his disagreements;

To John Frame and Jay Adams for teaching me that the Bible is practical;

To Bob Kramer whose friendship has so often been a channel of the grace of God to me;

To my family, Nan, Peter, Gwenyth, and Hannah, for their forbearance, love, and prayers during many long days;

To many brothers and sisters who prayed for both health and wisdom.

1

RECLAIMING SPIRITUAL WARFARE

SOME PEOPLE REALLY DO SEE A DEMON behind every bush. Cynthia, a woman I counseled, once cast out demons from her toaster when it failed to work![1] More seriously, she and her husband Andrew had a remarkable—and remarkably destructive—way of arguing with each other. For the first five minutes they warmed up with normal person-to-person bickering. But at a certain point, when the fighting turned nasty, they shifted gears and wheeled in heavier artillery. They would bind, rebuke, and attempt to cast out demons of anger, pride, and self-righteousness from each other.

In Cynthia's words,

> I saw the demon looking out of his eyes, glittering and murderous. So I said, "Demon of anger, I bind your power in Jesus' name!" Then I claimed the power of Jesus' blood as my cover from all demonic assault coming through my husband.

The result? Not only did Cynthia and Andrew reinforce their hostility, they trampled the name of Christ through the mud of their superstition, hostility, fear, and confusion. Needless to say, the real devil—who aims to dishonor God and conform us to his evil ways—could only be pleased at the ensuing personal and interpersonal wreckage.

Other people I have met grant the devil and his demons such mighty power that their working theology of human evil is "the devil made me—or you, or him, or her—do it." Janice's life, for instance, had long been characterized by selfish, hostile, fearful behavior. She had bounced from one group of Christians to another, from one deviant teaching to another. Janice attended a small group Bible study sporadically, and one night threw a tantrum when she felt snubbed by someone. James, a member of the group, proceeded to "take authority over Satan," attempting to drive demons of bitterness, self, and low self-esteem out of her. He later commented, "The tantrum wasn't really her talking. It was the demons inside her manifesting. The real Janice loves the Lord. The demons took advantage of old traumas and unforgiveness from her family to gain a foothold."

In other words, the devil made her do it. Janice, by the way, at first found this a wonderfully appealing explanation for her life of troubles. She frequented "spiritual warfare" ministries for a number of months, claiming deliverance from any number of demonic inhabitants. She thought her problems were really solved. But eventually this fad wore off too, and her life bumped along as usual.

Some people go so far as to view all the problems of life as demonically animated. Randy lived his "Christianity" as if the universe teemed with demonic agencies whose will and activity provide life's ultimate explanation and drama. He saw situational hardships—bad health, financial straits, meanness from coworkers—as demonic "mountains" (citing Mark 11:23) to "come against and cast out in warfare praying." Randy also personalized his own problems—temper, sexual lust, discouragement, overeating, loneliness—as demons of the respective sin or struggle that needed to be cast out in self-exorcisms.

Randy had been initiated into this worldview through a pastor who specialized in "spiritual warfare." When the pastor cast out Randy's "demons" of anger, rage, and disappointment, he had gone on a two-day high after being "delivered" from these sins-as-demons. Then on the third day he became irritated at a coworker. Immediately he thought, "Oh no, they're back." Subsequently Randy developed a continuing lifestyle of self-deliverance-through-spiritual-warfare, not realizing that it bears no apparent relation to what the Bible describes as the Christian life. Our secular modern age may have created a barren and dis-enchanted world, but an over-fascination with demonic agents creates a lurid, reenchanted counterworld that is just as bad.

Still other people see Satan as a second god, viewing life as an *ultimate* conflict between good and evil. Jeff assumed that the mental world of restless, vigilant fear he inhabited was Christian and objective. But actually his beliefs came closer to the old heresy called Manichaeism. He gave good and evil equal ulti-macy, rejecting the sovereignty of God over Satan and denying that God uses evil to the glory of his grace. Jeff professed that "Christ had the victory," for this is what he read in books and heard the teachers say. But in the trenches of life Satan and God fought for his soul as near equals; the outcome was always in doubt; his own will cast the deciding vote.

Jeff believed that like Vietcong infiltrators on a dark night, demons might slip into his personality and take over. If he let down his guard, if he failed to pray the right formulas, if he forgot to say the right words of power, spirits could—and would—crowd in. His salvation and peace were ultimately his own responsi-bility, depending on which rival power he yielded to moment by moment. Jeff converted truth and prayer into incantations. He had forgotten—or never knew—that "the devil is *God's* devil." And he had never learned that "salvation is of the Lord"; that the Father who begets us watches over us; that trust in the God who made and rules heaven and earth—including the devil—is often simple and peaceful rather than heroic and dicey.

Today, unfortunately, these cases are not oddities. A great deal of fiction, superstition, fantasy, nonsense, nuttiness, and downright heresy flourishes in the church under the guise of "spiritual warfare" in our time. For many people like Cynthia, Andrew, Janice, James, Randy, and Jeff, the working worldview of spiritual warfare has the ring of a horror movie or fantasy novel instead of the sound of Scripture. But the warfare we really need to wage engages and implicates our humanity, rather than bypassing it for a superspiritual, demonic realm.

For many reasons, cases like those cited above are multiplying. Clearly the time is urgent to reclaim true spiritual warfare.

REASONS FOR THE URGENCY

 Seven considerations underline this vital need. First, *we live in a society where the modern agenda has largely failed.* The Enlightenment vision held that human reason, science, technology, and good intentions could overthrow God and ignore the devil and still create good, happy people living in a good society. But that vision has turned into a moral nightmare. Moderns believed they could establish the true, the good, and the beautiful; postmoderns believe in nothing or anything at all. But as Christians living in the modern age we must reassert biblical vision and practice. We know that life is ultimately a moral conflict between good and evil, right and wrong, true and false, life and death, God and the devil. We must reclaim true spiritual warfare.

 Second, *we live in a society that has become increasingly pagan.* With the death of the belief that science could know all things and solve all problems, the spiritual world is growing in its influence. Occult thinking is on the rise, including astrology, New Age, Satanism, mediumship, Gaia, and resurgent native religions. A society fascinated with spirit powers also seems fascinated with violence and sexual perversion. Pagan beliefs are entertained seriously as viable and valid options. New Age thinking infiltrates education, business, and government. Our fantasy and entertainment life has taken on an occult cast with many books, games, songs, and movies that explore the demonic. People are becoming obsessed with things that God calls detestable. We must reclaim true spiritual warfare.

 Third, *missions, anthropology, and modern communications make us increasingly aware of the practices and beliefs of animistic cultures.* In our society occult influence is growing; in many others, however, it has long been entrenched as the dominant worldview. What used to be studied in anthropology courses is now mainstream through multiculturalism and the global village. The Bible itself was addressed into such a world rife with occult belief and practice. How should we understand and minister to people who experience life as a morass of spirit powers? We must reclaim true spiritual warfare.

④ _Fourth, we live in a society of high-profile bondage to "addictions,"_ such as alcohol, drugs, cigarettes, immoral sex, violence, food, work, television, exercise, money, pleasure, sports, and so on. The human tendency toward willing slavery has never had a more diverse supermarket of options. A heightened awareness of compulsively destructive and self-destructive behavior has now combined with the failure of standard solutions, especially in tough cases. Many ask why people are in bondage. Where we find slaves, are there not also slave masters? We must reclaim true spiritual warfare.

⑤ _Fifth, bizarre or troubled behavior, often related to experiences of extreme abuse, seems to be appearing more frequently._ Our society wallows in its atrocities and pathologies. "Multiple Personality Disorder," for example, has received a great deal of attention in the mass media in recent years. Such bizarre behavior is often associated with experiences of brutality, atrocity, and betrayal—sometimes real, sometimes imagined. In either case, how do we help these people living in extreme anguish, confusion, self-deception, bondage, chaos, anger, and fear? Is there a demonic component in this devastation of lives? We must reclaim true spiritual warfare.

⑥ _Sixth, many people have sometimes experienced an uncanny, heightened sense of the presence of evil._ Certain things, places, and people seem unusually dark. Perhaps it is a person with a malignant quality, an obsession with destructive powers, a brooding malevolence to God, or a manipulative, Bible-twisting, deceitful, chaotic lifestyle. Perhaps specific manifestations of evil seem explicable only as demonic presences. How can we explain and address such things? We must reclaim true spiritual warfare.

(7)   Seventh, *a growing number of Christians teach and practice "deliverance" ministry in the quest to cast out inhabiting demons.* This renewed interest in practical demonology and spiritual warfare has raised a host of questions: Are there demonized Christians? Territorial spirits? Demons inherited from ancestors? Demons of various sins? Demons as sources of information? Can warfare prayers bind, loose, and take authority over dark powers?

Frank Peretti, for example, has found an audience of millions for his vivid novels featuring demons and deliverance.[2] Should we read his books as engaging fantasies and evaluate them simply for their literary and imaginative merit or demerit? Or does Peretti mean his books partly as theology: true portrayals of how demons work and how to wage spiritual warfare? Many Christians believe—and live—the worldview of *This Present Darkness*, which is the worldview of many deliverance ministries. Do deliverance ministries deliver on their claim of successfully waging spiritual warfare? Or do they multiply questions that demand answers? We must reclaim true spiritual warfare.

Spiritual warfare is not only a hot issue, but a hotly contested one. This book will raise serious questions about the beliefs and practices of contemporary deliverance ministries. But in most cases I do not write about enemies, but about and to brothers and sisters—and even to friends. The enemy of our souls is our common adversary and we are not unaware of his schemes. Satan intends to spread division by inciting caricature, suspicion, lies, accusation, and hostility among God's people. After all, he is in the business of propagating himself in our attitudes and actions. And so although I will disagree—sometimes sharply—with several distinctive emphases of deliverance ministries, I would like to begin in a different key.

My Intentions

My interest in reclaiming spiritual warfare is not simply theoretical. Each of the seven reasons for the urgency has touched me personally. First, I was educated at Harvard during the late 1960s when confidence in modern science was dying painfully, and at the University of Pennsylvania in the 1980s when postmodern relativism was firmly in place. Second, I have interacted with neopagans and witnessed the deluding power of the arch liar in their lives. Third, a missions stint in Uganda brought me face to face with witchcraft, animism, and forms of semi-Christianity that verged toward the occult and ecstatic. Related to the fourth and fifth points, I have encountered people in all sorts of trouble as I worked in a psychiatric hospital for four years during the early 1970s and now as a counselor for the past fifteen years: the bizarre, the miserable, the evil, the confused. Sixth, on several striking occasions I have experienced the presence of uncanny evil, incidents that bore the marks of direct demonic malice. And seventh, the issues of demon-deliverance ministry have been controversial in my own church, and I have interacted extensively both with practitioners and recipients of deliverance.

I must add an eighth factor as well. I have experienced in innumerable ways the power of the Holy Spirit and his Word to bring light into darkness, freedom from bondage, sanity where there was confusion. I do not write as a detached, abstract theologian, but as someone who believes and bears witness to the practicality and power of the Bible's practical theology.

What centered my prayers during the process of writing was: "Give me love for you, Lord, and submission to what you say. Give me love for those about whom I will write. Give me love for those who will read." I have thought often about Paul's exhortation in 2 Timothy 2:22–26 as a guide to godliness amid controversy. For our Lord wills that we pursue what is good with a pure heart, doing all with *praotees*. The Greek word means that we should do all with gentleness, meekness, humility. *Praotees* captures the quality of a horse responsive to the will, hand, and bridle of its master. Whether at full gallop or a slow walk, whether turning right or left, the rider's hand guides. *Praotees*[3] speaks truth in love.

The sinful opposites are easy enough to identify, though hard to shake. They are among the devil's chief ends. In the midst of controversy it is easy to become headstrong, opinionated, judgmental, argumentative, uncharitable, abrasive. It is just as easy to become timid, tentative, people-pleasing, waffling, compromising. Our enemy's supreme goal is to exert moral lordship. He sabotages both truth and love if he can conform us to his image. Our Lord's goal is also moral lordship, making us like Christ himself by the power of the Spirit and the truth of the Word. Writing this book has been a skirmish in the larger spiritual war. I hope that I have succeeded in truth, in love, in humility.

Reading, too, is an activity that involves spiritual warfare. You will listen, question, evaluate, and act. Your opinions and attitudes, like mine, lie open before the Searcher of hearts. I hope my readers succeed in truth, love, and humility. I hope you read carefully, patiently, thoughtfully, and charitably. I hope you are critical in the best sense rather than the worst sense. I believe that the way you read and respond can bring glory to our Lord and help the body of Christ grow in wisdom.

My goal in writing is to offer a clear, biblical, pastoral, practical point of reference—not that everyone will agree with me all the time. But I hope that everyone will engage the questions honestly, wrestling with what the Bible actually teaches us to believe and do. I do not expect to be proven right on every issue. This book may contain errors, omissions, and infelicities that will need correction. But after much study, prayer, reflection, and discussion, I believe that the general direction of the argument is sound and biblical.

Truly all Christians believe in spiritual warfare; we all believe that Christ delivers us from evil. But as I write I will seek to answer two crucial points of confrontation regarding spiritual warfare. The first question engages how we understand the Christian life. *What are we fighting?* How does the evil one actually work? How does he exert—or attempt to exert—his dominion? The second question engages our practice of the Christian life. How should we fight? What is the way God delivers us—and tells us to deliver ourselves and each other—from bondage to the devil? *What is the mode of warfare?*

I will not seek to be exhaustive, answering every vexed question. But I will seek to answer these two questions biblically and persuasively. This is a vital need, because the vast majority of contemporary books on spiritual warfare give incorrect or inadequate answers to these two questions. My goal will remain focused, so in many places I will simply pass by important questions or only allude to important truths. I trust the reader will look other places to fill out the details. But my argument will give a cogent point of view that will suggest the direction to take on many details not covered here. It could have a cascading effect on the wisdom, power, and depth of the mutual aid, prayer, and counsel that occur within the body of Christ. I lift my prayers to that end.

The church of Christ—denominations, local churches, and even families—is divided on these questions. We each tend to see our view as the balance point, seeing Christians on one side of us as embracing the Enlightenment's empty rationalism, and seeing those on the other side as embracing fanaticism. I do not exempt myself from this phenomenon. But when real differences coexist within large areas of agreement, I hope we can create constructive conflict. Speaking the truth in love, we will grow up together.[4] Ideas and practices can and must be battled over and discussed. Clarity and conviction make wonderful companions for charity and humility.

OUR COMMON GROUND

As I have said, this book will critically evaluate contemporary deliverance ministry teachings with the intention of proposing a sounder, more biblical view. But first we must establish areas of common ground among today's Bible-believing Christians on the topic of spiritual warfare. The large majority of Christians give assent to four propositions, whatever our other differences. The first two propositions are matters of Scripture and basic worldview. They derive from how we interpret the Word. For all who are Christians, they come with the territory. The third and fourth propositions are matters of contemporary application. They derive from how we interpret the world. Although most thoughtful Christians will agree on the answers, the scope of agreement may vary.

First, *we are involved in a spiritual warfare*. Christians—in fact all human beings—take sides in a world war. God and God's people face off against adversaries in this world under malign spiritual rule. This world war had a beginning, has a middle, and will have an end. We are now in the midst of a fire fight. We are "in action," actors in the theater of war.

Our opponent, the lord of darkness, is variously named and described as adversary, evil one, enemy, accuser, devil, Satan, slanderer, god of this world, serpent, dragon, murderer, liar, and tempter. In the Bible Satan rarely appears for long on center stage because our moral drama is front and center. But just often enough we glimpse backstage and see the devil ruling his hosts, both human and demonic. His people include false prophets, murderers, unbelievers, cowards, fornicators, drunks, enemies, oppressors, and all whom Scripture says will not inherit the kingdom of God. They include lovers of money, pleasure, human approval, and self.[5] Such people oppose God's rule and God's people. And Satan's demons oppose all people—even his own—because his kingdom is a kingdom of slavery and tyranny, tortures and betrayed promises.

We should understand all history as spiritual warfare. The Bible portrays human history as a drama of war and peace. The two chapters in the beginning speak of God's creation, of time before war came, of paradise. In this short-lived peace, God sets the stage and defines the terms of the ensuing conflict: good or evil, life or death, God's authority or any other. The other is yet offstage.

War begins in Genesis 3 and the enemy advance continues through the rest of the Old Testament to the gospels. All-conquering evil obliterated peace and life. Satan ruled the nations and most people walked in blind unbelief, diverse sins, and death. But the sovereign God took a people for himself from the midst of the dominion of darkness. A thin strand of resistance, faith, and promise preserved a challenge to the dominion of sin and death. The lawful King said that he would come some day. The "poor and afflicted" lived in this hope of a Deliverer from sin and death.

God revealed his face of glory during the time when the world was without hope and without God. But sorrow and failure hung over even the most godly human lives. Noah, who walked with God, also shamed himself as a drunk, and he died. Abraham, God's friend, also jeopardized his wife's purity because of fear, and he died. Jacob, whom God loved, also connived for the very gifts that God had freely promised, and he died. Moses, who spoke face to face with God, also forfeited the promised land in a fit of anger, and he died. Samson, the great deliverer, also was a fool for love, and he died. Job, the man who feared God and turned from evil like no one else on earth, also needed to repent of his self-justifying pride, and he died. David, the man after God's own heart, also committed adultery and arranged a murder, and he died.

Utter evil ruled the hearts of humanity at large. Certainly flashes of light and goodness appeared in the lives of the seed of promise, but so did moral compromise. And death pronounced the final word on everyone, both the wise and the foolish. Then at the end of this line of promises not yet fulfilled, of groaning and disappointment, of imperfect and wandering people doomed to die, came the perfect man.

Thus our second shared proposition is that *Jesus Christ is the triumphant Deliverer and King.* Jesus, the pioneer and perfecter of faith, the Lord of glory, brings light and life. He is the man over whom Satan could gain no control. The Son of God loved his Father with no sinful remainder or qualifier, and he lives.

The life, death, resurrection, and ascension of Jesus Christ reversed the tide of war. This King appeared, single-handedly breaking the stranglehold of the oppressor. Christians believe Jesus' words that his death and resurrection will cast out the devil: "Now judgment is upon this world; now the ruler of this world shall be cast out. And I, if I be lifted up from the earth, will draw all men to myself" (John 12:31–32, NASB). Jesus speaks of his cross as the definitive cosmic exorcism. This event—the only exorcism in the gospel of John—breaks Satan's hold over the world. And all Christians believe in deliverance: "For he has rescued us from the dominion of darkness and brought us into the kingdom of the Son he loves" (Colossians 1:13).

We experience deliverance from the power of Satan when we turn consciously from darkness to the light.[6] The one who blinds us that we might wallow in lies, lusts, and misery is sentenced to everlasting darkness, while we who once lived in fear of death now rise to life in hope of the resurrection. Through the Holy Spirit, we are in Christ and Christ is in us. As freed captives we are learning to love our King and are unlearning the ways of our former oppressor and master. Death and sin no longer have the last say.

When the enemy was on the offensive, flashes of light appeared in the darkness. Now Christ is on the offensive, yet shadows of evil linger in the light. We still live by promise; we still live mixed lives; we still face the prowling enemy of our souls; we still face the last enemy, death. Everything is not yet under Jesus' feet.

The tide of battle, however, has turned and the balance of power has shifted. Invading light and glory now weigh more than the remaining darkness and evil. And God gives his people effective weapons for the warfare we must fight: we must be delivered from the power of the evil one by believing, praying, repenting, obeying, seeking, and serving. Jesus taught us to pray, entreating God to "deliver us from the evil one."

God promises a final day when peace will arrive forever. In two chapters at the end of the Bible, we glimpse warfare ended, paradise regained, enemies destroyed, and God living amid his people.

As we have seen, Satan appears on stage or backstage throughout the central period of history. But his power to rule, deceive, tempt, torment, and accuse was fundamentally broken. In the final act, our enemy and his human and demonic servants will vanish into the lake of fire forever. But we still live in the conclusion of war. The conflict between the seeds of woman and serpent lies at the heart of our life's drama on this dark planet until the morning star rises. These first two points state needed affirmations; the next two points state ways of understanding our times.

③   Third, *the modern age deadens people to the reality of spiritual warfare.* Most Christians would agree on this. Much of Western intellectual life in the past two hundred fifty years has been dedicated to demythologizing God and the devil, good and evil. The practical atheism of modern intellectual life has made reality to be fundamentally material and social, not spiritual. Belief in the devil is seen as a primitive curiosity, the resort of people ignorant of the real forces—chemical, neurological, psychological, sociological—that play out in human life. To modern skeptics and unbelievers, religion is a comforting opiate or a self-serving illusion; the devil and his God are dead for those with eyes to see.

Science, technology, and medicine reinforce this dominant ideology that only the "natural" world exists. Can a modern believe that God controls lightning and thunder if a meteorologist can use satellite pictures and computer modeling to predict the storm a week ahead of time? Can a modern believe that demons could cause paralysis, seizures, or deafness if an EEG and electromyogram can map patterns of electrical impulse in the nervous system? Can a modern believe that a personal tempter engages our wills in a contest between good and evil if particular configurations of DNA or one's family history seem to correlate to a higher incidence of drunkenness or sexual perversion? A devil of the gaps becomes as irrelevant as a God of the gaps when the perceived gaps in human competency shrink.

The modern world presents us not only with skeptical ideas and beguiling efficacies but also embeds us in social structures that argue against the Bible's God and devil. In a postmodern pluralistic society that tolerates and upholds a multitude of world-views, who can believe that a conspiratorial being animates and proliferates lies, opposing the one, eternal, universally binding truth? When individuals each arbitrate their own truth and morals, all is relative and all authority is suspect. Both God and Satan, as figures of authority, are absurd in a context that enforces diversity as the only truth, and an absolute as the only error. And God and Satan are equally irrelevant if religion is relegated to private life, making no impact on politics, business, or scholarship.

The ideological, technological, and social forces of modernity corrode belief in spirit beings. At best the devil is a mythical representation of social or psychological forces. Our times make belief in a spiritual war implausible to many, and this modern mentality easily infects Christians. For some professing Christians the devil has about the same practical status as Santa Claus. Perhaps he lingers on as a point of abstract doctrine, but in practice Enlightenment thinking has exorcised him far more effectively than Jesus ever did.

Downplaying or demythologizing spiritual warfare usually creates a pernicious domino effect. Prayer and worship become hollow forms. God's power and aid are little needed and little expected. Sin becomes psychopathology or social maladjustment. The Bible becomes a remote object, not the voice of the living God. Evangelism becomes vaguely embarrassing; death to self is distastefully fanatical. Normal life becomes, well, normal: work and unemployment, marriage and divorce, sickness and health, the economy and politics, traffic jams and weather, war and peace.

As biblical Christians, however, we deny that this secularized rationalism makes up the Christian faith. Normal everyday life is charged with importance. We know that there is warfare to be waged, and we do not deny the existence and work of our foe.

Fourth, *errors and excesses occur in deliverance ministries*. Most Christians will agree with this proposition as well. We need not listen long nor read far before encountering practices, ideas, and experiences that career into the bizarre—and the sad. The examples at the beginning of this chapter highlight some of the problems. Thoughtful advocates of deliverance ministry agree, and deplore such things.

If deadly rationalism saps spiritual vitality on the one hand, the exorcistic mentality spawns mutant spiritualities on the other. Both the disenchanted world of modern rationalism and the charmed world of premodern spiritism are wrong. Liberals often graft Christian elements onto an underlying naturalistic world-view, creating a hybrid religion perhaps acceptable to modern minds. Similarly, the deliverance mentality often grafts Christian elements onto an underlying demonic and superstitious world-view, creating a hybrid perhaps acceptable to premodern minds. But the biblical Christian faith needs to stand alone; it should not be grafted onto any other worldview.

OUT OF ONE DITCH AND INTO ANOTHER

Many practitioners of "spiritual warfare" have a good impulse and good intentions. They clearly see the ditch on one side of the road—the follies of the modern age—because they recognize that the Christian life is about spiritual warfare. And they want to help troubled people. But too often they swerve into the ditch on the other side of the road, because the proper curbs are not built into the deliverance-ministry worldview. In rejecting the modern secular worldview they often succumb to the "old pagan" worldview in documentable ways. The more sober practitioners are as troubled as I am by the cases recounted at the beginning of this chapter. But they see such things as excesses—distortions of a fundamentally sound paradigm. I believe that these cases, however, are actually extensions—logical outworkings of a fundamental unsoundness in the paradigm. But that debate lies in the chapters ahead.

2

WHAT IS
SPIRITUAL WARFARE?

THE NEEDS OF OUR WORLD call for true spiritual warfare to be reclaimed. But how should we answer the call? In broad strokes, three competing visions vie for our allegiance. The first vision I will dismiss out of hand as inadequate to all serious followers of Christ: capitulation to the spirit of the age by radically reinterpreting the Bible's "spirit" realities as mythical projections of psychological, sociological, political, economic, and medical phenomena. The second vision, encompassed by the demon-deliverance ministries, will engage much of our attention. I will next describe these ministries at some length, interacting with their teachings and methods. Although I will describe the third vision—the "classic" Christian mode of spiritual warfare—more briefly at first, it will also play a significant role. But first we will turn to the demon-deliverance approach to spiritual warfare.

THE "EKBALLISTIC MODE" OF SPIRITUAL WARFARE

Many contemporary Christians have responded to the vital need to reclaim spiritual warfare by resorting to "deliverance" or "warfare" ministries that seek to identify and cast demons out of believers. What should we call this movement? I used the reasonably accurate term "demon deliverance" above because the defining distinctive of all these ministries is their goal to deliver Christians of evil spirits. But "demon deliverance" is not quite

27

specific enough for my purposes, for when Jesus delivered people from demons he actually did something quite different from what the current deliverance ministries typically do.

How about "exorcism"? Very few in contemporary deliverance ministries like or use the term. The Greek root word occurs in only one place in the New Testament—Acts 19:13. And even there it does not describe Christian ministry, but Jewish magic practice that undergoes a humiliating defeat. In addition, the word has overtones of paganism, sensationalism, or empty ritualism. Exorcism is also associated with the idea of "demon possession." Modern demon-deliverance ministries do not use this phrase as a description of "demonization," for they assert that Christians cannot be "possessed" by the devil because they belong to God. But they would say that Christians may be "demonized" to a greater or lesser extent when held in bondage to sin by indwelling spirits. To label these ministers as exorcists of the demon possessed would be pejorative and not reflect their self-understanding.

These ministries typically describe themselves using the words *deliverance, warfare,* or *spiritual warfare*. But all Bible-believing Christians believe in deliverance, warfare, and spiritual warfare, and many disagree with the distinctives of "deliverance" ministries. These ministries assert a particular version of spiritual warfare that has developed in recent years. Whether their version is correct or faulty is precisely the point of debate as we reclaim spiritual warfare. In doing so we should not relinquish good words whose meaning is at stake.

I will describe the demon-deliverance movement using an invented term that might seem awkward at first glance. But it will carry the freight and highlight the distinctives that most need serious debate within the body of Christ. I will use the term "ekballistic mode of ministry," with the acronym EMM for short. Ekballistic comes from the Greek word *ekballo*, which means to "cast out." From *ek*—out—we get "exit." And from *ballo*—to throw or cast—we get "ballistic." A ballistic missile is "thrown" into its trajectory and then falls in an arc as gravity pulls it.

In the gospels when someone suffered an unclean spirit, Jesus showed mercy by casting it out. The practice of casting or driving out spirits captures the most distinctive feature of contemporary deliverance ministries, or EMM. Proponents say that Christians and non-Christians often require an "ekballistic encounter" to cast out inhabiting demons that enslave us in sexual lust, anger, low self-esteem, substance abuse, fascination with the occult, unbelief, and other ungodly patterns.

The term EMM focuses on the *mode of ministry*, suggesting a particular form of pastoral activity: casting out demons. It is part of a grassroots practical theology—a way of addressing life problems—that finds varied expression both in pastoral ministry and in methods of personal growth. Ekballistic evangelism, for example, seeks to drive demons out of people and places so that individuals and groups can come to Christ who would otherwise be prevented. Ekballistic sanctification seeks to break demonic strongholds inside Christians; "when the demon goes, the Christian grows." EMM sanctification can be done to others as part of discipleship-counseling. And Christians can do it to themselves after being taught methods of ongoing self-deliverance. In sum, ekballistic spiritual warfare envisions the warfare of Christians as a battle against invading demons, either to repel them at the gates or eject them after they have taken up residence.

Contemporary EMM is obviously based on the key assumption that demons of sin reside within the human heart. According to EMM advocates, people undergo a moral demonization. For example, indwelling demons of rage, lewdness, terror, pride, rebellion, and accusation reinforce—and in some way control—anger, immorality, fear, self-absorption, obstinacy, and self-recrimination. Demons take up residency and, to a greater or lesser extent, take over functions of the human heart. As squatters in the soul, they exert the power of a behind-the-scenes government.

In EMM thinking, to suggest that someone may be having a "spiritual" problem is to suggest that it may be a "spirit" problem: unclean spirits blind the understanding, enslave the will, and explain why an otherwise well-meaning Christian seems powerless to change. Such "demonization" is not seen as a global takeover—as "possession"—but as a pocket of alien inhabitation within the human personality. We could use the metaphor of the human personality as a computer hard disk with demons acting as computer viruses. These viruses can overwrite and corrupt sectors of the hard disk, executing their own commands within those sectors. Such demons must be removed; EMM is viral protection software.

Proponents say that demons gain access—a "ground"—in several ways. One is through our own sins. Such habitual sins as immorality, anger and unforgiveness, and addiction to drugs, alcohol, or food can give demons a foothold, which they can then solidify into a stronghold. Or occult practice and cultic objects can draw demons. Strong emotions in childhood, such as fears or anger, can become occasions of demonization. Also the sins of ancestors—for example, occultism or immorality—can beset the present generation with inherited demons. Or the direct sins of others against us, such as physical, sexual, Satanic ritual, or emotional abuse, can provide an entry gate for unclean spirits. Such spirits may cause us to repeat the same sins, to grovel in self-blame and low self-esteem, to live enslaved to reactive bitterness, fear, and escapism, or cause various physical afflictions. The drama of human life is seen as a "spiritual" drama: infiltrators and invaders cluster around, looking for grounds to penetrate the defenses of the human personality. Such is the diagnosis for which EMM is the treatment.

Doing EMM

Many variations of the basic EMM methodology exist, but I will describe a generic version. Usually a troubled person seeks help because some form of public teaching awakens the concern that one's life problems are rooted in inhabiting spirits that have not been recognized or dealt with. Or a troubled person may be brought to the EMM expert by concerned friends and relatives who think there may be a "spiritual component."

A counseling process begins. Often the minister or counselor takes time to get to know the person, gathering such background information as prior involvement with the occult or specific sins. A family history is usually taken. Often the minister introduces the subject of demonization as a possibility, teaching the basics of ekballistic spiritual warfare. An extended time of prayer might follow with the counselor claiming certain promises and protections and "coming against" evil powers. The person would be called to renounce sin patterns and involvement with occult activities.

After this time of prayer, possible indications of inhabitation by demons are seen in the residue of bondage or the obsessive thoughts that remain or manifest themselves. Perhaps the person shows marked boredom or an antipathy to prayer. Or the counselee may experience thoughts, impulses, emotions, memories, and fantasies alien to his or her conscious volitions, beliefs, and self-image. For example, someone renounces anger and prays to forgive a parent but experiences some disturbing and otherwise inexplicable remnant of fierce bitterness or unforgiveness.

At this point the counselor may suspect that indwelling demons control parts of the person. It is time for an ekballistic encounter. The EMM practitioner will seek to identify demons by name through inviting them to manifest, through a direct revelation, or through the counselee's free associations. Some effort is often made to identify the "ground" by which demons gained entry into the person's life and the "right" by which they maintain residence. Such conversation may occur with either the person or the demon.

The actual encounter with the demons then takes place: the minister takes authority over them, binds them, and commands them to leave in Jesus' name. In less dramatic forms of EMM, the counselee is simply invited to believe and affirm biblical promises while praying certain prayers against the evil spirits. In some power encounters there are such physical effects as sneezing, coughing, shouting, bizarre voices, vomiting, and convulsions. In others, the counselee might simply report a sense of relief. After the ekballistic encounter, basic discipleship follows as the way of "maintaining one's deliverance." The person may be taught techniques of auto-EMM—various prayers, formulas for taking authority over dark powers, biblical truths to repeat—in order to stay free of demonic influence.

FOUR VARIETIES, ONE MOVEMENT

The EMM view of spiritual warfare has been developing since the late 1960s, with four prominent varieties. They all share fundamental common features but diverge in various particulars of both teaching and method. Authors frequently cite one another across the spectrum, usually favorably. Although there is intramural skirmishing on secondary matters, they are close enough in their distinctive emphases to be considered one movement.

Charismatics were the first popular exponents of this new view of spiritual warfare. Pastor Don Basham's best-selling *Deliver Us From Evil* in 1972 created enormous interest and notoriety. Basham teamed with other well-known charismatics, such as Derek Prince, to publicize this approach widely. The theology was crude and developed as the movement grew. Talkative demons lurked behind every bush and the fireworks were spectacular. This version of EMM continues, for example, in the ministry of Benny Hinn. Members of the other three varieties of EMM often testify to going through a similar stage of a fascination with demons and bizarre power encounters.

Dispensationalists developed the second variety of demon-deliverance ministry. A pointedly noncharismatic approach arose in the circles around Dallas Theological Seminary and Moody Bible College. Authors of well-known books include Mark Bubeck (*The Adversary*, 1975), Merrill Unger (*What Demons Can Do to Saints*, 1977), and Fred Dickason (*Demon Possession and the Christian*, 1987). This variety has a more restrained feel, operating more through private pastoral counseling and prayer than through extraordinary encounters with demons. They articulate their theology more clearly than the charismatics in a style heavy on lists of proof texts.

A third variety has arisen in what has been called the "third wave of the Holy Spirit," centering around Fuller Theological Seminary. Well-known leaders include John Wimber, Peter Wagner, Charles Kraft, John White, and Wayne Grudem. Well-known emphases include "signs and wonders," church growth, and third-world missions. This variety is characterized by a comprehensive and systematic theological rationale that centers on the coming of the kingdom of God and a strong concern for multicultural evangelism. The notion of "territorial spirits"—ruler demons that hold entire cities or regions in bondage to unbelief and sin—is a recent innovation within third-wave teaching.

A fourth variety might be characterized as broadly evangelical. Neil Anderson (Freedom in Christ), Timothy Warner (Trinity Evangelical Divinity School), Tom White (Frontline Ministries), and Ed Murphy (OC International) have all recently written books weaving features of EMM thinking into a more traditional evangelical perspective.[1] Anderson is probably the most popular author now. His approach is distinctive for its pronounced general self-help emphasis, but he has wisely distanced himself from the flamboyant "power encounters," and has instead emphasized truth and faith as aspects of self-deliverance from demon inhabitants.

Novelist Frank Peretti has his own special place in the EMM movement. The world he portrays is most like the early charismatics: demons lurk everywhere and the confrontations are spectacular. But he also grants a significant role to territorial demons. Peretti makes a sharp divide between demonized non-Christians and Holy Spirit-filled Christians. His demon deliverances are not woven into the subtleties of the sanctification process as they are for some of the more counseling-minded authors listed above.

My purpose here is not to distinguish the differences between approaches but rather to interact with the common features. I will describe a generic version of the demon-deliverance ministry; my comments will not always apply to every author, teacher, or practitioner. It should also be said that the teachers mentioned may not endorse everything that happens within the movement they helped set in motion.

Let me also say from the outset that—as with most movements—there is a spectrum from the relatively more balanced and sober to the relatively more unbalanced and, in some cases, bizarre. Examples of outrageous theological errors and egregious mistakes in pastoral care and self-understanding would be easy to pick out. But to some degree the movement has policed its own by self-criticism. It is neither monolithic nor static. I hope that this book, as a voice from outside, will contribute to constructive self-criticism within the movement.

Many practitioners point to a maturation process that pruned out the rash enthusiasms of youth. Both individual practitioners and the movement as a whole have actually drifted *away* from ekballistic encounters. As they mature, most EMM practitioners seek to arouse fewer fireworks, such as demon manifestations and talking to demons, instead engaging in more talk to responsible human beings. This movement seeks to take the Bible seriously; whatever the remaining flaws may be, the Lord's hand can be discerned cutting back the brush of demon hysteria.

Ekballistic practitioners tend to move *toward* a hybrid of EMM and the classic mode of spiritual warfare, sometimes with a dose of psychology/psychiatry stirred in.[2] The EMM distinctives still naturally tend to excite the greatest attention, however, and the fundamental assumptions remain. I will focus on neither the worst nor the best, but on the common.

The ekballistic vision of ministry, personal growth, and spiritual warfare is not the only possible vision. In the history of the evangelical churches it is actually a radical and recent innovation. The long dominant view is what I will call the classic Christian mode of ministry in spiritual warfare.

The "Classic Mode" of Spiritual Warfare

Most Christians who have written on the issue of spiritual warfare throughout history have not taken the EMM point of view. They have described the inworking power of Satan to produce human bondage to sin and lies without demonizing sin. Thus the classic mode of warfare—of evangelism, discipleship, and personal growth—has followed the pattern of Jesus facing Satan in the desert. The textbooks for spiritual warfare in this mode have been the Psalms and Proverbs, the ways that Jesus addressed moral evil, and the teachings of the New Testament epistles.

Puritan pastoral theologians, for example, wrote frequently and with great depth on spiritual warfare. As they wrote about Scripture, the devil, and human nature, they were alert to the incredible evil and deceptive strategies of Satan. At the same time they made a heart-searching analysis of the human condition. The Puritans were not demythologized moderns; they lived in a spirit-filled world and were well aware of spiritual warfare. They saw the combat, snares, deceits, and schemes of Satan, but did not employ an ekballistic mode of ministry. Books still in print after over three hundred years include Thomas Brooks's *Precious Remedies Against Satan's Devices*, John Bunyan's *Pilgrim's Progress* and *Holy War*, and William Gurnall's *The Christian in Complete Armor*.

Numerous modern Christian authors have written about spiritual warfare in a non-EMM vein as well. C. S. Lewis's *The Screwtape Letters*, *The Great Divorce*, and the space trilogy articulate the devil's immoral suasion and cruelty while never demonizing sin or positing a solution that casts the demons out. Such popular pastoral theologians as Ray Stedman, Jay Adams, and John MacArthur, writing more didactically, also call Christians to the sturdy forms of classic-mode spiritual warfare.[3]

Two other influential authors need to be mentioned in connection with the classic mode. EMM advocates often assume that if bizarre possession phenomena occur, then EMM is automatically the way to respond. But John Nevius and Frederick

Leahy were two pioneering thinkers who addressed demon-possession phenomena, especially on the mission field, without turning to casting out demons. Nevius, a Presbyterian missionary to China in the nineteenth century, is often considered the founder of modern practical demonology because of his book *Demon Possession and Allied Themes*. He reported hundreds of cases of demon possession among the Chinese but used the classic mode to deliver them. Leahy, an Irish Presbyterian, wrote *Satan Cast Out* in 1975 because he was concerned about the number of books on demonology that "pay scant attention to the Biblical evidence, pander to the sensational and often arrive at unwarranted conclusions."[4]

The leading elements of the classic mode of spiritual warfare are best captured by Ephesians 6:10–20: reliance on the power and protection of God, embracing the Word of God, specific obedience, fervent and focused prayer, and the aid of fellow believers. Spiritual warfare with the power of evil is a matter of consistently and repeatedly turning from darkness to light in the midst of assailing darkness. Christians fight spiritual warfare by repentance, faith, and obedience. Recognizing the powerful influence of Satan within the human heart, classic-mode pastoral theologians have not called for ekballistic evangelism, ekballistic sanctification, or ekballistic protection from the powers of evil.

EMM's Strengths

There is one final introductory matter to raise—the strengths of EMM. The best of contemporary "spiritual warfare" ministries have six positive aspects. First, they recognize and challenge the spiritual barrenness—the practical atheism—of the secular modern age. We all need to hear this message, as we can be easily seduced by our culture's technological and managerial efficiency.

Second, they encourage conservative Christians to reenvision the world as a spiritual place so that the fight for Christ's kingdom and glory might be more effective. To live and pray as if seeing invisible realities is at the heart of Christian life. In reminding us of invisible powers—both God and the enemy—they challenge common perversions of the classic mode of warfare that seem in practice to underestimate the forces of darkness and the forces of light.

Third, they challenge the notion that people's personal problems can be reduced to purely psychological, social, physiological, or circumstantial factors. Instead, when we understand what is really wrong, we will recognize a raging spiritual debate for our souls: Which king rules, God or the evil one? Truly the human soul is contested ground. Christians are not invulnerable to drift, sin, apostasy, error, or evil. The Christian life is not a Sunday drive on the interstate with air conditioning and cruise control. The Shepherd of our souls personally leads us along a road with bumps, twists, pot holes, traffic jams, blizzards, wrecks, precipices, wash outs, erroneous road signs, and even terrorist attacks.

Fourth, many "spiritual warriors" demonstrate admirable love and self-sacrifice. I have known and read of men and women who give vast amounts of time and energy freely out of compassion for struggling people. They seek to help the addicted, the confused, the depressed, the angry. Many are willing to "get their hands dirty" in real problems as they weave awareness of spiritual warfare into both pastoral care and evangelism. This example of sacrificial ministry has both humbled and challenged me.

Fifth, they show that prayer matters. If our warfare is indeed "spiritual," then we need what God alone can do. To be strong in the strength of the Lord means to pray: dependent, persistent, bold, biblically guided prayer. I appreciate their often burning concern to pray and rely on the Lord. This deep commitment rebukes the feeble prayers and feeble theology that so often reveal a Christian sleepwalking on the battlefield.

Sixth, they usually believe and practice classic-mode spiritual warfare much of the time. Prayer, awareness of warfare with the power of evil both within and without, love for the Word, and love for needy people are all characteristics of alive Christians.

But some features of the recent resurgence of interest in spiritual warfare are not so good. Some aspects, in fact, are downright dangerous to the church's view of God, sin, the devil, the Christian life, prayer, and ministry. Zeal without knowledge can tear down and confuse the body of Christ rather than strengthen people in grace.

These six strengths do not make contemporary deliverance ministries unique, for they are actually old biblical truths updated. At their best, they bring us back, afresh, to John Bunyan's *Holy War* and *Pilgrim's Progress*. But the "new truths" and "distinctive teachings" of modern deliverance ministries are more problematic and need to be explored.

3

ASK QUESTIONS OF THE TEXT IN CONTEXT

WHAT DOES SCRIPTURE SAY about demons and deliverance? How *should* we fight spiritual warfare? Questions arise because one group of people committed to Scripture disagrees with another group also committed to the same Scripture. Where is our court of appeal? Can we establish ground rules for fresh and productive engagement with the Word of God—and with each other? How should we use Scripture to understand and reclaim spiritual warfare? How do we gain the mind of God? How do we build a comprehensive and practical understanding of God's ways of war? Identifying principles of sound Bible interpretation is a key component of listening to the word of truth.

THE BIBLE SPEAKS TODAY

The key is to ask questions of the text in context. The Bible addresses our real questions, needs, concerns, and problems. God always speaks concretely into situations of human need; no book of the Bible was written as an exercise in abstract theory. But we do not read the Bible in its original settings—wandering in the Sinai desert as nomads, for example; few of us wrestle with grumbling if no oasis appears on the horizon. Nor do we live as cosmopolitans in first-century Corinth; few of us wonder how to live a pure life amid Aphrodite's ritual prostitutes and food sacrifices.

39

Today we ask different questions; we face different struggles, concerns, troubles. Scripture, however, presumes that it speaks to us and to our valid questions too. For instance, when Paul wrote the Corinthians, he said that the ancient desert wanderers served as examples for sophisticated first-century people because their particular struggles and temptations were common to all people, always, everywhere. In this case, Scripture itself (1 Corinthians) models how to apply other Scripture (Exodus and Numbers) to diverse human questions. Similarly, if we perform the interpretive task well, the book of Numbers speaks to children grumbling over a plate of leftover tuna casserole and Paul's letter to the Corinthians speaks to a former homosexual still drawn to pornographic videos.

In the same way the Bible speaks to the many questions surrounding spiritual warfare in our day. We must ask our questions and listen well for answers. The list of valid questions is nearly endless. For example, some people come to the Bible asking very personal questions: "I dabbled extensively in the occult and was immoral before I was converted. I've changed, but I can't seem to shake angry thoughts at God and lustful fantasies. I hate these things, but I feel helpless when the feelings come over me. What's the connection to my past lifestyle? Am I demonized by spirits of lust and occult power? Do I need a power encounter to set me free of residual bondage?" These are valid questions. And the person struggling with them will read the Bible with such questions on his or her mind while doing so.

Consider another example. Many EMM advocates encounter other Christians who largely ignore the devil, dismiss attention to spiritual forces as needless or fanatical, and suggest that God's love automatically insulates them from danger or harm. When they meet this type of Christian, some EMM advocates wonder, "Does faith create an immunity to demonic attack, or can a believer be seriously harassed by the devil?" So they read Job, the gospels, Ephesians, 1 Peter, and Revelation with the question in mind. And they conclude rightly, "Faith helps us take God's shield for protection from fiery darts. God does not transport us instantly into a paradise off limits to the devil."

Both the Bible and our experience show that believers can and do suffer misery, temptation, accusation, and bondage to habitual sins; the devil plays a part. But quite often EMM advocates go further and conclude that such afflictions are a sign of demonization, thereby necessitating EMM. But is this further conclusion warranted? We must look at Job, the gospels, Ephesians, 1 Peter, and Revelation for answers.

THREE KEY TASKS

Scripture will answer the valid questions we ask. Of course Scripture does not answer every question our curiosity may generate, such as the following questions about spiritual warfare: How did Satan become evil? How did demonized people become demonized? EMM advocates respect that the first question is a mystery, but speculate about the second. Scripture, however, never says a word about causes of demonization. Plainly we do not need to know how the Gadarene demoniac got that way, because it is not important for faith and practice, for ministry or personal growth in grace. The Bible will answer the questions we need to know to live to God's glory instead of being bound in sin.[1]

There are three intertwining tasks in the process of asking questions of the text: first, listen to the text; second, grasp the context; and third, ask your questions. My order does not reflect an order of importance, for all three tasks are crucial and occur simultaneously. But my ordering seeks to avoid several pitfalls. On the one hand, if our questions overwhelm both text and context, we never quite listen to God's corrective word. Popular or personal opinion, prejudice, impulse, and tradition will dictate answers, obscuring questions we ought to ask. On the other hand, if the context overwhelms the particular text, we may hear some general biblical truths but the specific truth we most need may be obscured or overwhelmed. The text must have the first say.

First, *let the text speak for itself*. We must listen for specifics. What does this passage actually say? Images come to mind as I think of this task: get as *near* as you can. Sit in the front row. Climb into the shoes of the speaker and listener. Stop. Look. Listen. What does the Holy Spirit intend to teach by this part of Scripture?

Ask the right questions—clarification questions that put your ear closer to the text, not *your* questions imported from outside, which you should ask later. "Let the text speak for itself" reminds us to be attentive, submissive listeners to a purposeful speaker. Listening is a skill with vast spiritual implications: "He who has ears to hear, let him hear" (Mark 4:9). Like any skill it demands concentration and will be rewarded.[2]

Second, *grasp the context*. Step back and look at the immediate setting of any passage: the surrounding sentences, the drama, the actors on stage, any details that are mentioned, any conclusions that are drawn. Why are these here? How do they help us listen better to the text? Look at the larger frame: the flow and intentions of an entire book. Look at the panorama: the sweep of the entire Bible. Statements about Satan and spiritual warfare do not lie scattered randomly, like fallen leaves on the lawn of Scripture. The leaves live on trees, connecting to larger purposes and patterns.

Remember the old maxim, "A text without a context is a pretext." The Bible can be made to say anything we want—if we ignore what it *does* say. After all, the Bible itself tells us, "There is no God" (Psalm 14:1). But that text changes in meaning when we look at the surrounding verses. Without alertness to context, we can lose important nuances of truth and sometimes major themes.

Third, *ask your questions*. The text is the leaf and the context the tree, but without the question and the questioner, texts and contexts remain curiosities—photographs of trees in an old textbook. Our questions bring about action: ask, seek, knock, dig, explore, listen, look, smell, taste, touch, notice. "Who is God? Who am I? What should I believe about this? What should I do when that happens?" Scripture is written to answer real human questions—and often to awaken us to the real questions. "What must I do to be saved?": people alert enough to ask this will pay attention. "Lord, teach us to pray": the request expresses a question, the living sense of need for help. "How long, O Lord? Where are your former lovingkindnesses?": when darkness seems to have the high hand, people who love light awake from their slumber. "Should I expect to discover—and then cast out—demons of anger, fear, lust, unbelief, and lies?"

These questions matter. We cannot be content with simply hearing what Scripture *had* to say back then to those people over there. We must hear what it *has* to say to us here and now. The word of God is "living and active . . . it judges the thoughts and attitudes of the heart" (Hebrews 4:12). What was written in former times is also for *our* instruction now. "Ask your questions," because built into Scripture is the expectation of proliferating applications.

When these three tasks are combined, we gain an increasingly sharp ear for what Scripture intends us to hear. As we do so we will grow confident that we hear what God says to his people. Real progress in reclaiming spiritual warfare occurs when combining these tasks generates an open discussion and exchange. My own thinking and development, for example, has been profoundly influenced by others through conversations and books. The EMM movement has challenged and stretched me, even where I end up disagreeing with it. I have been challenged by the development within EMM thought: John Wimber's associates and Neil Anderson make a more convincing and nuanced case for EMM in the 1990s than Don Basham made in the 1960s. But they have yet to address the fundamental weaknesses in EMM distinctives. My hope in this book is to contribute to a sharpening of the church's wisdom in the great war with evil.

FLATTENING AND FRAGMENTATION

Listening well to the text means that we will explore and probe specific passages about Satan, demons, and spiritual warfare.

Looking at the context means that we must look at everything that surrounds and embeds those passages. After all, no book of the Bible is *about* Satan, for the Bible is *about* human beings before the face of God. And asking questions means we will address the need of God's people to reclaim spiritual warfare. How do we resist the devil and grow in godliness? How do we understand and tackle the hard cases? What do we make of the distinctive EMM teachings?

When we fail to question the text in context, we do not hear what God says—we become hearing-impaired. This metaphor resonates with me because from birth I have been deaf in one ear. I miss many things that people with two good ears hear. Stereo music? The direction of a voice calling from somewhere in a crowded room? Sounds outside at night, when the good ear is next to the pillow? A whisper in the (wrong) ear?

We all have an instinctive hearing impairment regarding God's voice. The new birth gives "ears" to those who formerly heard the voice of the world, flesh, and devil but were stone-deaf to God. But having been reborn, we must spend the rest of our lives learning to hear better. For all of us, individually and corporately, some things simply do not yet register. When we fail to question texts in contexts, we miss what is there, and Scripture becomes fragmented and flattened.

Fragmentation occurs when context is lost. Bible verses become marbles in a bag rather than threads in a tapestry. Consider that, in the customary way we divide things up, the Bible contains about thirty thousand verses. Dividing the Bible into chapters and verses is, of course, only a convention and convenience. Moses, David, Ezekiel, Luke, and Paul simply wrote books, prayers, and letters—with no chapters and verses. Chapters make the most sense in Psalms, and are logical to separate the speeches in Job and the reigns of Israel's kings. Verses make the best sense in alphabetical passages (such as Psalm 119) and such a collection of material as Proverbs 10–31. But on the negative side, dividing books into chapter and verse probably reinforces the habit of fragmenting the Bible into discrete "marbles," harming our sense of context and overall unity.

Of the Bible's thirty thousand verses, hundreds mention Satan, demonization, and evil spirits. Should we view Scripture as a bag containing thirty thousand marbles of various colors? If we do, we would learn about Satan by locating and culling the scarlet marbles. Put all the scarlet marbles together and we would have our theology of Satan.

But in fact, *all thirty thousand verses bear on our understanding spiritual warfare.* The scarlet passages are threads within a single, unified tapestry, composed of many smaller designs. Through his words God teaches us to understand who he is, who we are, who the enemy is, and the nature of our current conflict.

Contexts are significant: Scripture is composed of passages within books within an Old and a New Covenant. Its passages are not marbles—unconnected fragments—that we can isolate and line up in arbitrary order. God's speaking embeds particular comments and incidents within larger interpretive themes.

For example, as we understand the *reasons* why Jesus did ekballistic ministry and the particular sorts of *problems* he addressed by this ministry, we will understand something important for determining whether we should use EMM in waging spiritual warfare. These reasons and problems are detailed in the context of each ekballistic encounter. Lose the context, and Jesus' ekballistic work simply sits in the bag next to Job 1–2, Ephesians 6, and Revelation 13. Gain the context, and the text tells us what we formerly did not hear.

The second problem—flattening—occurs when the distinctives of the particular passage are lost. What a passage means to teach us becomes obscured; some lowest common denominator blinds us to its details. Sometimes flattening occurs when other contexts in the Bible are imported. For example, EMM literature often exports the ekballistic encounters from the gospels into the rest of Scripture, overwhelming what Ephesians 6, James 4, 1 Peter 5, and Revelation *actually* say about spiritual warfare. Flattening can also occur when something is imported from outside the Bible. For example, many EMM books teach that the human heart can become a haunted house of demons inherited from sinful ancestors, which is not what the Bible itself says about the human heart. The notion of ancestral spirits is a bit of occult theology read *into* the Bible, not *out* of it.

Usually fragmentation and flattening occur simultaneously. The twin errors of fragmentation and flattening both lose the systematic riches of Scripture. For example, Job strikingly portrays how Satan's malice is constrained by God's sovereignty and how God will be glorified. Yet Job is also the longest, most wrenching, and most personal expression of the *human* dilemma in the entire Bible. EMM books tend to highlight Satan's torment of Job. They may mention in passing that God is in control, but they do not really hear the text or see the context of Job. The EMM mentality rightly identifies Job as someone afflicted by the dark power. But it fails to do justice to Satan's subordination to God, the integrity of the human dilemma in suffering, and the over-arching purpose of the glory of God.

Fragmentation and flattening are both dangers of "proof-texting"—we are neither close enough nor far enough away from the Bible to hear and see what we should. When we make this mistake, the text stops speaking for itself, illuminated by the context. Texts then tend to become verbal inkblot tests, patterns of words into which we pour our own opinions, pre-interpretations, experiences, and concerns. When the interpretive task missteps, it is as if we hear only snatches of a conversation, filling in the blanks with our imagination. We do not let the Bible speak for itself, according to God's purposes.

FICTION OR FACT?

Consider an example of what happens when a passage of the Bible is isolated from its context. Millions of people have read Frank Peretti's novel, *This Present Darkness*. Peretti adopted his title from Ephesians 6:12: "Our warfare is not with flesh and blood, but . . . against the world rulers of this present darkness"

(RSV). Peretti picked a logical passage from which to derive the title of his novel. Ephesians 6:10–20 is the most focused description of spiritual warfare in the entire Bible, heaping up descriptions of the forces of wickedness. In Peretti's telling, this present darkness comes to life, teeming with graphic and even lurid detail. Demons cluster around, invade, and inhabit human beings. And Peretti's heroes use EMM for waging warfare.

In fantasy, the attributes of demons and the ways of war are fair game for the literary imagination. As fantasy Peretti is often compared with J. R. R. Tolkien's *The Lord of the Rings* or C. S. Lewis's space trilogy. For Peretti, as for Tolkien and Lewis, fiction does not mean false. Vivid fiction can wake people up to reality. "There's a war going on for my soul! I better wake up from sleep, repent of living indifferently, pray fervently to the Lord, and live life by his grace to his glory!" Peretti can do that for people. He did it for me.

But as with Tolkien or Lewis, trouble comes if readers take the details of their working theology from an imaginative work. Ringwraiths and orcs are clearly metaphorical demons. Magic wands and spells are clearly metaphorical weapons. Similarly, Peretti's dark angels are a provocative invention—maybe. We know Tolkien does not "mean" his ringwraiths and wands to correspond to systematic biblical theology. But we are not so sure how much Peretti "means" his demons and EMM methods to inform our actual worldview and practice.

Peretti's readers also get into trouble if they read into Ephesians 6 the ideas and mode of ministry that appear in the novel. Ephesians 6:12 does indeed describe evil spiritual powers. But Ephesians nowhere teaches that demons control people through invasion and inhabitation. Ephesians teaches something far more ominous in scope and depth. And Ephesians 6:10–20 nowhere teaches EMM in the way that Peretti does. It teaches us a different, more powerful, and more human way to fight.[3]

So if Peretti has written pure fiction, then his title is fine, as it simply sends the reader provocative and imaginative signals. Peretti can write about fantasy spirits and fantasy weapons in any way his imagination leads. But if his book is taken as theology—giving us a demonology, a practical theology of warfare, and a true interpretation of Ephesians 6 warfare—then his title is wrong and misleading. It fragments and flattens the text.

Together we can reclaim spiritual warfare—far better than I can alone—as we heed the counsel in this chapter to ask questions of the text in context. Adopting a careful method of interpretation will not guarantee agreement on every vexed and vexing question, but it will help the body of Christ prune away many of the more dramatic errors that now claim to be biblical forms of spiritual warfare.

CULTURES DARK
WITH THE OCCULT

WISDOM IN SPIRITUAL WARFARE is a vital requirement in our time for good reasons, one being the rise of occult activity. When the demonic and the occult grow pervasive in a society, as they have in ours, human life unquestionably darkens and is degraded. Under the boot of evil, people suffer, become evil themselves, and die. This is part and parcel of what the Bible calls the dominion of sin over human life.

EMM practitioners agree with this, but give a unique twist to occult involvement. It opens up people, they say, to spirits that infiltrate and control the personality and must be ejected by ekballistic means. Of the varied theories about how people come to "have an unclean spirit," the notion of occult involvement is the most widespread. Repentance, renunciation, faith, and putting on a new lifestyle are not deemed sufficient to clean out the interior strongholds; a power encounter with the resident demon must take place.

In this chapter we will examine whether this understanding is biblical and give first say to the text. Because the Old Testament was addressed to a world alive with the occult, we turn to it first to determine the Bible's view.

A DEGRADED EXISTENCE

The period of history in the Old Testament was an age when the nations lived without hope and without God.[1] In the ancient

Near East occult beliefs and practices were so dominant and pervasive that whole societies lived in darkness under the power of Satan. They worshiped idols, believed lies, and lived in bondage.

God planted Israel in the midst of three cultures: the Canaanite, Egyptian, and Babylonian. All three cultures teemed with demonic agents and activities, with belief in demons and demon worship, with possession phenomena, exorcism, spiritism, and other sordid practices. Israel was created to be light in this omnipresent darkness, but the nation continually interacted and intermingled with these cultures. More ominously, God's people were repeatedly corrupted by spiritual evil. Sometimes even the king indulged in the worst practices, such as the notorious Manasseh who did it all.[2] It was said he even did "more evil" than the surrounding nations because he sinned against the light whereas they sinned in the darkness.

There are three important features of this occult worldview and its degraded existence. First, demonological explanations for all events and actions—good or bad—predominated. People had to win favor with the local demons, spirits, and gods or appease them in order to receive blessings. They credited unappeased demons with causing everything from a broken pot to falling ill to disappointment in love to defeat in war.

Second, occult idolatry and practices were the norm. Astrologers, pagan priests, diviners, mediums, sorcerers, ecstatics, and soothsayers abounded. Numbing brutalities occurred, such as child sacrifice in worship to Molech. Sexuality was grotesquely perverted through ritual prostitution. Children were raised to worship demons by their parents and by entire cultures that practiced abominations.

Third, nations that practiced the occult also pursued other generic human addictions, such as gluttony, drunkenness, varied forms of immorality, greed, blood thirst, and power. Israel herself often succumbed to this moral degradation.[3] This entire world—including Israel at times—also suffered from the afflictions that attended the dominion of darkness: infectious disease, locusts, drought, famine, carnivorous animals, and the devastations of war. The world of the nations, often including Israel, teemed with spirits, gods, idols, demons, sin, and death.

Interestingly, these varied sins and traumas are what contemporary EMM advocates identify as the "grounds" by which demons of sin enter our lives to hold us in moral bondage, necessitating EMM: occult practice, habitual sin, ancestral iniquity, abuse, and so forth. We will discuss the suggested causes of demonization later, but at this point we should note an important point: All the contemporary "causes" are in place in the Old Testament, but the Scriptures never identify or address spirit inhabitants as the problem nor cast them out as the solution. From the perspective of Old Testament law there was no solution, only the penalty of death. But there are examples of occultists who repent, believe, and change their ways in the classic mode.

The Old Testament, as a voice into these demon-filled cultures, exhibits two striking features. First, it minimizes Satan. It neither endorses the testimony of the nations to the occult worldview nor accommodates itself to demonological explanations for human sin or most human suffering. Instead it gives an altogether different view of the devil, evil spirits, God, and the nature of our warfare. We could even say that the Old Testament unmasks the occult worldview as mythical, so that we might not be diverted from the real battle with evil and the evil one.

Second, the Old Testament maximizes human responsibility. Even the most profoundly degraded conditions are rooted in the human heart, not inhabiting demons, as the following passages show.

> The LORD saw how great man's wickedness on the earth had become, and that every inclination of the thoughts of his heart was only evil all the time (Genesis 6:5).

> In those days Israel had no king; everyone did as he saw fit (Judges 21:25).

The hearts of men, moreover, are full of evil and there is madness in their hearts while they live (Ecclesiastes 9:3).

The heart is deceitful above all things and beyond cure. Who can understand it? (Jeremiah 17:9)

These two features—reducing the role of demons and emphasizing human depravity—have striking implications for today's mode of warfare with evil.

LIFTING THE CURTAIN

The Old Testament features the LORD and his people on center stage. But every so often God lifts the curtain to show the spirit realities at work behind the scenes. Six major passages in the Old Testament allow us to glimpse backstage: Genesis 3, 1 Samuel 16, 1 Samuel 28, 1 Kings 22, Job 1–2, and Zechariah 3. Scripture freely acknowledges evil spirits, but as we will see as we examine each of these passages, its teachings are opposed to the occult worldview. They also stand at odds with leading features of the popular EMM worldview. Pick up your Old Testament as we look backstage.

Genesis 3:1–15

God opens the curtain wide at the very entry point of evil. We learn of three crucial matters: Who is Satan? What is the nature of our warfare? What are the consequences of spiritual defeat? We will consider each in turn.

The Bible's teaching about Satan begins in Genesis 3: "Now the serpent was more crafty than any of the wild animals the LORD God had made." Notice how Scripture pointedly and repeatedly rivets into our consciousness the fact that God is Creator and Satan is creature. Satan comes as a *serpent*—a created being. He is explicitly compared to *wild animals*, which the LORD God *made*. Scripture repudiates the ultimate dualism of the pagan worldview—the view that forces of good and evil are equal at the highest levels. The repeated mention of Satan's physical form shows him as a creature rebelling against the Creator who holds power over him.

Genesis 3:14–15 reinforces this theme as God delivers the curse on Satan. Again Satan is compared to animals, not to God. In addition, the serpent is unmistakably subordinate as he is brought to accountability and cursed by God. He will be defeated by another creature, the seed of the woman, a man whom God has promised.

God's sovereign authority and power over Satan could not be emphasized more strongly. Satan is on our side of the Creator-creature divide; he is only the false god of this world. He plays out his malice on the stage of the earth, but his works on the earth will be destroyed. He exists at God's forbearance, to fulfill God's purposes. In the occult worldview, the demons have an independent existence. But right from the start the biblical worldview shows that evil spirits are radically subordinate to the Almighty, who alone is God.

Notice, second, the nature of our warfare. Satan is malicious, a liar and a murderer. He himself is morally evil and is judged as such. He tempts, deceives, and seeks to rule Adam and Eve, conforming them to evil. The core issue of human life is defined as a *moral* issue. Who will rule our hearts? Whose voice will we listen to? Who will we believe? Trust for blessings? Obey? To whose will does the "eargate" open?[4] Will we prove obedient creatures or disobedient, good or evil?

Third, suffering, affliction, torment, accusation, and death are *consequences* of our moral dilemma, and are not unjust. The problem of sin is the ultimate *cause* of all our varied miseries. Those who listen to the serpent's voice will feel the serpent's fangs. We will return to this crucial issue of cause and consequence in subsequent chapters. At this time simply note that Genesis 3 lends no support to EMM distinctives. It opposes dualistic tendencies and does not demonize sin.

1 Samuel 16:13–23

David is anointed king of Israel and the Spirit of the LORD departs from Saul, having come on David in power. At the same time, an evil spirit begins to torment Saul. David is brought to comfort Saul with music and drive away the spirit. Four times (16:14, 15, 16, 23) the evil spirit is specifically called an evil spirit *from the* LORD or *from God*. God used the evil spirit to accomplish his twofold purposes: first, he judged Saul's rebellion by sending a tormentor; second, he exalted David by allowing David to bless Saul with peace. In the chapters that follow, David is revealed as a Christ-like king, a man after God's own heart, against whom Saul rages. Again, as in Genesis 3, the powers of evil are radically subordinate to the LORD. Perhaps this passage even hints at the anointed one's power to dispel those afflicting spirits that cause human misery, a temporary alleviation of the pain of God's curse on sin.

EMM advocates frequently use this passage to discuss whether believers can be demonized. But the question tends to devolve into inconclusive speculation: Was the demon-harassed Saul one of God's people or not? Some EMM advocates say that Saul seems to exemplify that sinning believers can be demonized and therefore that EMM will help deliver them from bondage to sin. But this question misses the point of the passage for two reasons.

First, the demon is linked to God's *punishment* of sin, not to the power of sin. The demon does not make Saul sin, as if it had gained a "ground" through Saul's rebellion. Notice that Saul's rebellion is even compared to occult sins—divination and idolatry (1 Samuel 15:23). If serious sin is an entryway to moral demonization, we would expect Saul to have a ruler demon named "Rebellion" who would be implicated in the subsequent downward spiral of Saul's sin. But there is no such ruler demon. The spirit tormenting Saul is a consequence of his own sin. Although he lived chained within Satan's moral dominion and therefore experienced misery, he was not demonized in the EMM sense.[5]

Second, this particular passage offers no prooftext for EMM as the mode of ministry to employ with the demonized. On the contrary, David uses music therapy to bring Saul relief. As David played his harp—perhaps singing psalms of worship to the LORD—Saul was refreshed and the evil spirit departed from him. The passage shows the fundamental relationship between God and the demons, and perhaps hints at the classic mode of spiritual warfare. But it quickly stops any Israelite—or modern—who might drift into a demonological explanation for problems and sins.

1 Samuel 28:3–25

This passage describes the sordid world of occult practice, not evil spirits per se. When Saul became terrified as the Philistines assembled for battle, he secretly visited a medium. She shocked even herself by raising up the spirit of Samuel. Samuel pronounced God's curses to Saul's devastation. In this, the longest Old Testament passage showing the occult underside of life, God used a forbidden practice to accomplish his ends. This does not represent a softening of God's attitude toward the occult—mediums were to be killed because spiritism is an "abomination."

Notice that Saul's trafficking in the occult does not open a way for demonic control of his mind; rather it incurs wrath. The Bible says that the LORD killed Saul for rebelling and for consulting the medium (1 Chronicles 10:13–14). Yet God himself actually used this evil practice to bring the prophetic curse against Saul: God allowed the spirit of a godly man to return, via mediumship, as his agent.[6] The lesson is unmistakable: the LORD controls all things, even the utterly detestable. God used the witch of Endor as his instrument, even as he had spoken his word through the sorcerer Balaam four hundred years earlier. The occult is deeply evil, but God is thoroughly in control of evil.

1 Kings 22:6–28

The kings of Judah and Israel, Jehoshaphat and Ahab, had allied in order to fight Aram and were seeking prophetic confirmation for their plans. Four hundred prophets claimed they would be victorious, mounting a pep rally for the war. But the two kings wanted to hear from the LORD and finally prevailed on Micaiah for the truth. As Micaiah pronounced God's curse on Ahab, he opened a window onto heaven. The LORD had asked the assembled spirits, "Who will entice Ahab into attacking Ramoth Gilead and going to his death there?" A spirit volunteered to be a lying spirit in the mouths of the four hundred prophets. Micaiah concludes, "The LORD has put a lying spirit in the mouths of all these prophets of yours. The LORD has decreed disaster for you."

In this passage notice that the LORD initiated the conversation to control events. He actually employs something evil— lies, from a presumably evil spirit—in order to accomplish his greater purposes. This does not mean that the lying spirit was forced to act contrary to its nature; it was a liar and deceiver seeking to kill a king of God's people. Nor does this mean that the false prophets were not responsible for their words; that they had demons named "Liar" inhabiting them; that an ekballistic encounter by Micaiah might have delivered them from bondage to lies. In the spirit world, the LORD, "whose eyes are too pure to look on evil [and] cannot tolerate wrong" (Habakkuk 1:13), can employ wicked beings—themselves damnable—as agents of his judgment.[7]

Job 1:6–2:10

This is the fifth Old Testament passage to reveal the evil spirit at work backstage in the human drama. As the story unfolds, Satan seeks to prove that Job is ultimately self-serving and will curse God if life becomes hard for him. God first grants Satan permission to destroy Job's children and possessions. Then he allows Satan to destroy Job's health and employ his wife to tempt him.[8]

EMM advocates often cite Job to prove that Satan can directly afflict and tempt believers. They draw the further implication that therefore EMM must be part of the solution to our problems. Job 1–2 certainly proves that Satan can harm us. But it also opposes the EMM worldview and methodology.

Notice, first, that God is in control; he interrogates Satan and sets him up with leading questions. Satan must give an account for himself. He only speaks when spoken to, only acts within God's permission, and always has his malice channeled to God's glory. Satan's evil intent is unquestionable—he desires to defame God and brutalize Job, spurring Job to curse God. Yet he is strictly limited within God's permissive will. God will be glorified through the integrity of Job's life and struggle.

Second, notice that in spiritual warfare the human drama is a *moral* drama, not a demonological drama: Will Job curse God? Job's developing fidelity to God is demonstrated before the principality and power who had mocked the power of righteousness. The Bible never demonizes sins, turning people into puppets. Job is not inhabited by a cluster of demons named Self-righteousness, Pride, Despair, Anger, Self-pity, and Sarcasm. Rather he was a righteous man who was sorely tempted.

Third, notice Job's mode of spiritual warfare. Job actually never mentions Satan, the secondary cause of his afflictions. Nor does he focus on the tertiary causes: murderous raiders and thieves, painful sores covering his body, rejection by his wife and relatives. Instead Job wrestles with God, the primary cause, because God is sovereign. And finally Job repents of self-righteousness. He proved to be the wise spiritual warrior by honesty, by reproving his wife's and counselors' folly, by repentance, by faith. In so doing, Job glorified God and humiliated Satan.

Of course Satan touches and influences God's people in many ways, both by temptations and afflictions. But we need not choose between an airtight insulation from the devil and potential moral inhabitation by demons. We need not choose between a vapid, formal Christian faith and EMM. The human moral drama—the question of either being faithful or unfaithful to God, amid whatever temptations and sufferings—always remains a *human* moral drama.

Spiritual

Zechariah 3

Zechariah sees Joshua the high priest standing before the angel of the LORD with Satan standing at his right hand to accuse him. Joshua is unclean. But, interestingly, Satan is not even allowed to speak. The LORD takes Joshua's filthy rags and clothes him in the garments of righteousness. Satan acts as malicious accuser of a man who is sinful and justly accusable, a "burning stick snatched from the fire." But God the deliverer silences Satan with his stunning promises of the forgiveness of sins through a coming Messiah. The familiar themes are all present: Satan's evil-doing is boxed in; sin is the great problem; the coming Christ will deliver us from the penalty and power of our iniquity.

GOD'S SOVEREIGNTY IN AN EVIL WORLD

These six curtain-lifting passages in the Old Testament teach us to understand both the unlimited malice and the limited power of the evil one. God paints a remarkable and consistent picture, showing that the one who utterly enslaves the nations in the darkness of evil and death is a predictable, supporting actor in the larger story of God's holy love and holy wrath. Evil-spirit beings exist within the sovereignty of God's purposes to redeem and judge responsible human beings.

The stunning lesson is that God uses wickedness: Satan, evil spirits, false prophets, the evil of Joseph's brothers, Chaldean oppressors, Judas. What the wicked mean for evil, God works for good. God uses the evil of the evil to demonstrate his justice and purify the righteous. He uses the evil of the righteous to demonstrate his mercy and to define the terms of our ongoing spiritual warfare.[9]

This truth of God using evil for his glory pervades the Old Testament treatment of evil, whether spiritual or human, to the comfort of God's people. The Old Testament may not speak often about the devil and his stratagems, but it anchors our worldview and teaches us how to understand and fight spiritual warfare in the classic fashion.

I have yet to speak with or read an EMM advocate who articulates this understanding of God's sovereignty in the midst of evil. Consequently, their understanding of spiritual warfare becomes skewed. The demons become increasingly autonomous; sin becomes demonized; the world gains the look and feel of superstition rather than biblical wisdom.

EMM advocates repeatedly—and rightly—state that Christians need not fear the devil, though his malice may cause us harm and danger. But because they lack a true understanding of God's sovereignty, their reasons for courage do not stand. The "name of Jesus" too often is used as a charm in a world teeming with demons who act independently of God's providential rule. EMM advocates rightly seek to reestablish a worldview that recognizes spirit beings, both good and evil. But the drift in EMM thinking toward demonological explanations creates a world more precarious and spooky than the Bible's world. In this demon-filled world human vigilance must strike the deciding blow in the battle. Ironically, in the end, the EMM worldview has more affinities with the occult worldview than the biblical.

The Bible gives an opposite, theocentric explanation. There the love of God—love for his name's glory and his people's welfare—strikes the deciding blow in the battle. We take refuge in our shepherd's care, learning vigilance, putting on his armor, and strengthening our arms with the strength of his might. Psalms and Proverbs are the supreme manual for spiritual warfare, for fighting both flesh-and-blood and spiritual enemies. Knowing that the devil is God's devil brings us incalculable joy and confidence in battle with our adversary.

We learn in the Old Testament that the way to deal with idolatry, astrology, mediumship, sexual immorality, anger—the besetting sins of the demonological jungle—is to repent or die. People need repentance, faith, truth, prayer, and fidelity.

Scripture does not ignore evil, Satan, or demons. God fiercely warns against them all, commanding us to flee the abominations of child sacrifice, soothsayers, mediums, spiritism, paganism, sorcery, and astrology. When the prophets speak to idolaters and those involved in the occult, they preach repentance and faith, not EMM. Naaman the Aramean was an idol worshiper who came to faith through a little girl and Elisha. Hosea simply called idolatrous Israel to turn back to God. The Ninevites—members of an occult culture—believed God and repented at the preaching of Jonah. In no case, even with gross and occult sins, was the problem defined as inhabiting spirits needing ekballistic ministry.

A DIFFERENT MODE

In conclusion, the Old Testament teaches a worldview and method of fighting spiritual evil that is essentially different from EMM. First, there is a radical focus on the LORD—God is at absolute center stage. He is the one whose will controls all the affairs of people and spirits. Even when the Israelites were corrupted by demonistic cultures—sacrificing children, worshiping idols, becoming involved in mediumship—the LORD alone remains at center stage.

Second, human beings are always responsible moral agents and share center stage with God. People are responsible for their own evil, including occult involvement and idolatry. The Old Testament does not point to the demonic to account for human evil, bondage, and darkness. The creature Satan can lie and murder, but he cannot make people something less than human. The seed of the serpent, the Satan-ruled person, remains fully responsible.

Third, although the Old Testament acknowledges the activity of Satan and his demons, it shows that God is sovereign and the demons are constrained. The Creator's power carefully circumscribes the creaturely activities of Satan and the evil spirits. This stands in striking contrast to the surrounding occult worldview where demons have an independent existence and the forces of good and evil exist in a potentially equal combat.

The Bible's message to people in occult cultures is not simply that the Lord has greater power than the spirits, but that he uses the spirits to his purposes. Scripture destroys the notion of the haunted universe.

Fourth, God's sovereignty has striking implications for the Old Testament's mode of spiritual warfare, mode of ministry, mode of living the godly life, and mode of fighting multifaceted evil. Occult involvement was standard; degrading addictions abounded; uncanny evil haunted the world. But the mode of warfare that God taught was having faith in the Word of God, fearing God, turning from evil involvements, taking refuge in the LORD, and obeying his voice. EMM is never the mode of warfare. The demonological explanations and ekballistic solutions put forth by EMM advocates are actually closer to the pagan-occult worldview than the Old Testament's view.

When we look at all these Old Testament passages in context we see that the first thirty-nine books of the Bible decisively undercut EMM. But next we will turn to the central arguments in favor of EMM: the example of Jesus and his disciples in Matthew, Mark, Luke, and Acts.

important chapter

SIN AND SUFFERING

WHEN WE TURN THE PAGE from the Old Testament to the New, we enter a world of spiritual warfare that appears very different at first glance. Was the demonological worldview correct after all? Did the Old Testament just not notice the sea of demons in which we swim? Satan and evil spirits appear frequently in this new world in face-to-face dialogue and conflict.

In the first three gospels, casting out demons—an ekballistic mode of ministry—makes up a significant part of Jesus Christ's work and ministry.[1] It also characterizes, to a lesser extent, the work of Jesus' disciples. Ekballistic ministry appears in four books of the Bible: Matthew, Mark, Luke, and Acts. These books naturally make the strongest case for—or against—the continuing use of EMM as a method of spiritual warfare.

Are there differences between the Old Testament and Matthew, Mark, Luke, and Acts? Between these four books and the rest of the New Testament? How do we understand these differences? What are the implications for how God calls *us* to wage spiritual warfare? These are the questions we will explore.

Beyond any question, both Jesus and the apostles cast out demons—in short, they practiced a form of EMM. As will unfold in our discussion, however, their theological worldview, their reasons for using ekballistic methods, their understanding of what it accomplished, and their methods differ from current practitioners in significant ways.

Proponents of EMM make two major arguments based on the fact that Jesus identified demons, heard them speak, and cast them out. They claim that because Jesus and the apostles cast out demons, we should do likewise. Although they cite other passages in the Bible—1 Samuel, Job, Ephesians, Revelation—such citations simply buttress arguments from the gospels. They also use a second major argument that is logically connected to the first, claiming that because EMM is not forbidden by Jesus or the rest of the New Testament, there is no reason not to use it.

These arguments may seem forceful at first: "Jesus and the apostles practiced EMM. The Bible never forbids it. Therefore we should practice EMM." Obviously we want to follow Jesus, doing what he did and living as he lived. Our Savior and Lord is our model for faith, life, and ministry. To oppose EMM seems perverse or, at least, to depend on an argument from silence. Is opposition to EMM based on prejudice against the supernatural? Does it come from a theology corrupted by naturalistic assumptions or from queasiness about encountering evil powers—or even God's power—beyond our control?

Against all such views, I will argue that the Bible does not teach us to wage spiritual warfare using EMM. Rather Scripture teaches us a different way to live the Christian life and fight our ancient foe. My argument comes directly from the gospels, builds cumulatively over the next two chapters, and is rooted in the text in context, not in proof texts. This chapter examines two different modes of warfare that Jesus used against different works of the evil one. Chapters 6 and 7 consider the reasons for Jesus' use of ekballistic methods and the applicability of EMM for us.

THE DOMINION OF DARKNESS ENTAILS
SIN AND SUFFERING

One key to understanding spiritual warfare in the ministry of Jesus Christ is to notice that he mounted a twin-pronged offensive against the powers of evil—against moral evil and situational evil. Jesus employed two modes of warfare to address two different facets of the evil works of the devil. Scripture and everyday speech use the word "evil" in two distinct ways, situational and moral. A passage from Ecclesiastes 9:3 illustrates both: "This is the evil [situational] in everything that happens under the sun: The same destiny overtakes all. The hearts of men, moreover, are full of evil [moral] and there is madness in their hearts while they live, and afterwards they join the dead." We both do and experience evil; the dominion of darkness is made up of sin and suffering.

On the one hand, evil includes the element of responsibility: it means sin, wickedness, iniquity, lies. This is moral evil—the evil people *believe* and *do*. This is what God meant when he said that Job "fears God and shuns evil." God abhors moral evil because he is holy.[2] But Satan's organizing passion is to draw us into moral evil, making us like him and ruling us. When the Bible says that the Son of God appeared to destroy the works of the devil, it means moral evil first and foremost.[3]

On the other hand, evil includes the element of consequences: it means suffering, hardship, unpleasant and harmful events, death. This is situational evil—the evil we experience. Job used the word "evil" this way when he cried out in agony, "Have I not wept for those in trouble? . . . When I hoped for good, then evil came" (Job 30:25–26). One distinctive of situational evil is that both God and Satan use it, although of course with opposite intentions. Satan's intent is to harm us, inflicting us with such situational evils, and ultimately to murder us. God employs and applies situational evil too, but because he is holy his intention is to chasten or curse sinners, purifying the faith of his people and judging those who rebel.

Obviously the two meanings of evil are closely linked. Moral evil causes situational evil; sin is the sting that causes death. Suffering is the consequence of sin in two ways: first, sin causes others to suffer; second, sin will be paid back justly with harm sooner or later.[4] Satan, of course, exploits both moral and situational evil for his evil purposes.

The overall picture is sweeping and majestic. Comprehensive evil—sin and suffering—defines the human condition and the human dilemma. Yet equally comprehensive good—forgiveness and blessing—defines the gift of God in Christ. God's mercy to sinners provides a forgiveness that is just and breaks the power of reigning sin—achieving moral good. God's mercy to the afflicted breaks the teeth of enemies and plants us in paradise—achieving situational good.

Moral versus Situational Evil

This distinction between moral and situational evil leads to a vital point. Clearly Satan is both a liar who provokes moral evil and a murderer who applies situational evil. And in various places his demons are described acting in both capacities. They are liars: Scripture warns of "doctrines of demons" and spirits that animate false prophets.[5] They are tormentors: Saul was vexed; others suffered blindness, convulsions, and the like. So when we encounter the unclean spirits that demonize people in Matthew, Mark, Luke, and Acts, we should ask what they are doing: Are they leading people into sin, hurting people, or both? Conceivably they could be liars; conceivably they could hold people in moral bondage; conceivably they could be tormentors; conceivably they could be doing it all simultaneously—as EMM advocates teach.

But Scripture's answer is clear and unexpected. God consistently portrays inhabiting evil spirits as *situational*—not moral—evils that hurt and abuse people. "All those who had afflictions [the sick and demonized] pressed about Jesus" (Mark 3:10, NASB). Demonization is in fact recognized and identified by its expression through miserable conditions, such as blindness, deafness, paralysis, dementia, and seizures. Sins, such as unbelief, fear, anger, lust, and other addictions, point to Satan's moral lordship, but *never* to demonization calling for EMM. People are victims of demonic sufferings, just as they are victims of lameness, blindness, or purely physiological seizures.

This explains why the demonized are included in the lists of the sick whom Jesus heals[6] and why the New Testament is so matter-of-fact about demonization. Demonization is not spooky or morally charged any more than fever, disability, and other afflictions are morally charged. Ekballistic work was done to alleviate suffering. For example, the woman with the crippling spirit is compared to a thirsty ox or donkey, tied up and needing to be taken for water (Luke 13:10–17). Jesus *heals* the demonized, just as he does the other sick. The result of an ekballistic deliverance is relief, peace, and the restoration of mental and physical capabilities. It does not lead directly to moral improvement, except as the miracle prompts grateful faith in Jesus.

We should note that sometimes in Scripture sickness *is* a curse on a particular sin, as with Saul's demonization. In the gospels, however, it more often appears as part of the general curse. Therefore Jesus usually approaches the sick from the angle of sufferers needing relief, not sinners needing repentance. He challenged the disciples when they sought a cause-effect link for the blind man in John 9: "Who sinned, this man or his parents?" The man was blind, Jesus said, that the works of God might be revealed, not that either he or his parents might be admonished.

The same is true of ekballistic ministry throughout the New Testament. God's glory and kindness are revealed; the demonized are never portrayed as culpable for their afflictions. This does not mean the sick—and presumably the demonized—are not sinners in addition to their affliction. See how Jesus treats the lame men in Mark 2:5 and John 5:14. Without repentance, faith, and obedience the temporarily healed will face far worse sufferings—a threat of hell. Without repentance, faith, and obedience the exorcised will face seven worse demons—also a threat of hell.

Clearly in the gospels a person "has" an unclean spirit the same way he or she "has" a fever, convulsions, or a paralyzed limb. Contrary to EMM teaching, unclean spirits are never implicated as holding people in bondage to unbelief and sin.

They are never portrayed as inhabiting and enslaving sinful parts of the human personality. Instead they are part of the curse that the loving Savior has come to reverse.

In today's climate of opinion the New Testament's emphasis is so novel that it is worth reiterating: *the New Testament never links demonization to moral evil in the person who has a demon*. New Testament teaching does not connect inhabiting demons either to patterns of sin in the demonized individual or to the impact of others' sins. The one exception to this proves the rule. On several occasions in the gospels demon possession is specifically linked to moral evil: Matthew 11:18; Mark 3:21–30; Luke 7:33, John 7:20, John 8:48–52, and John 10:20. But these are all cases of *misdiagnosis*. John the Baptist and Jesus are falsely accused of being morally demonized. Jesus was charged with doing evil, with blasphemous insanity. John was probably charged with fanaticism.

There are only two cases of demon-inhabited people in which demons might be construed as linked to moral evil: the Gadarene demoniac (Mark 5:1–20) and the Philippian slave girl (Acts 16:16–18). But in the former case Scripture emphasizes his bizarre behavior and restless sense of torment. He might have been socially unacceptable, demented, and miserable, but is Scripture emphasizing his sinfulness? Did the demons have as a "ground" some sin pattern in him or his family? In no place does the Bible warrant such speculations about why this man—or anyone—suffers a case of demons. In the case of the slave girl, Scripture emphasizes how annoying the girl's truth-speaking eventually became, but assigns no moral evaluation. Obnoxious behavior is probably not always sinful.

Sin is not identified as the cause of demonization; neither is demonization linked to perpetuating sin. How demonic suffering or inspiration might interact with the victim's sinful nature is never in view in the biblical accounts. One can imagine that the demons would tempt the Gadarene to anger, despair, and fear, and the slave girl to pride and lust for power. But Scripture does not dwell on sinful responses to demonization. The

demons—and EMM—are sharply separated from anything
related to the spiritual warfare with indwelling sin.

This point deserves pondering by all proponents of EMM.
Not a single example in the Bible shows Jesus or the apostles
using EMM to deal with moral evil. The indwelling unclean
spirits, like other forms of suffering, perhaps created conditions of
temptation to moral evil for the victims.[7] But we have no evidence that demonization was either caused by sin and unbelief or
that it had any bondage-creating influence to perpetuate sin or
unbelief.

DIFFERENT MODES FOR DIFFERENT EVIL

The next step is to see that Jesus Christ overcomes both forms of
evil—moral and situational—but each in a different way. Both
sin and misery are overcome through Jesus Christ. As the one
who "delivers us from the evil one" (Matthew 6:13), he has con-
quered both sin and death. He has removed both the power
(moral evil) and the penalty (situational evil) of sin. But we
must not move too fast and miss a key point: To destroy the
works of the prince of darkness Jesus used both the classic and
the ekballistic modes—each in its appropriate place.

In the beginning of Jesus' public ministry, Satan came against
him as a tempter to moral evil. Satan desired to rule Jesus' heart.
But Jesus used the classic mode to resist the devil, trusting in
God's word of truth and obeying through God's indwelling
power.[8] Similarly, when Jesus spoke to other people's actions,
beliefs, motives, and reactions, he called them to the classic
mode: repent, trust in God's word of truth, and obey through
God's indwelling power.

The lesson is clear: Whenever and wherever Jesus addressed
Satan's attempts to establish or maintain evil moral lordship, he
used the non-EMM, classic mode of spiritual warfare. He never
cast out demons of sin from people, but instead exposed and
reproved sin, inviting people to the God of grace.

It is when Jesus encountered sufferers—the sick, demonized, hungry, bereaved, disabled, poor, endangered, oppressed, and misled—that he often used a different mode of warfare. Against situational evil he wielded merciful power to deliver people and draw them to himself. In the case of the demonized, Jesus used ekballistic ministry. For other sufferers he brought similar relief through such things as healings and resurrections at a command, multiplying loaves of bread, and stilling the storm. Jesus often used the power mode to temporarily alleviate sufferings, giving a taste of freedom from the curse.

But Jesus also used and taught the classic mode in facing situational suffering. Although he suffered situational evils he did not use acts of power to reverse his own afflictions, such as turning stones into bread when he was famished. When Satan came against him as a murderer, Jesus suffered as the Lamb of God. His resurrection—the ultimate power act—was performed in the classic mode: he was obedient unto death, reliant on the promise of the Father's power to raise him up. "Now the ruler of this world is cast out," Jesus says, but the irony is stunning: the supreme ekballistic results were accomplished through the classic mode. He also taught the classic mode to his disciples in the Lord's Prayer. "Lead us not into temptation, but deliver us from the evil one" covers both our sufferings and our sins. In sum, Jesus always used the classic mode to deal with moral evil; he used both the classic and ekballistic modes to deal with situational evil.

A brief allegory will illustrate these two modes of addressing the two aspects of evil. Imagine the human armies of darkness as well-armed, dedicated, brainwashed soldiers who are barefoot, ragged, diseased, hungry, wounded, and oppressed by their officers. Against them the task of the armies of light is to fight in two modes, first destroying their moral evil and second doing them good to overcome situational suffering. The armies of light first drop bombs and leaflets on the soldiers. The bombs are to destroy moral evil: both the capacity and the will to fight. Some enemy soldiers will be killed; others will be wounded or demoralized. The leaflets promise life, food, clothing, good treatment, and so on to all who surrender. They can either give up and live or keep fighting and die. But so that the enemies will know that the army of light means well, the army of light makes airdrops of food, clothing, shoes, and medicine behind enemy lines. Life-giving supplies reinforce the leaflets, making the promises tangible by actually doing some immediate good. This temporary repair of situational evil is only a foretaste of the blessings of faith in the conqueror. But the leaflets contain a warning, too. If the bedraggled soldiers who experience a warm meal, new shoes, and antibiotics do not repent, even worse afflictions await them: eternal death and torment.

Jesus fought war both ways. The temporary airdrop was EMM, doing good to those who suffered within the dominion of darkness. The bombs, leaflets, and convoys of nourishing supplies were the classic mode. Together, the two modes utterly defeated both moral and situational darkness.

On the one hand, the gospels narrate one long "power encounter" between Jesus and the varied evils that harass people. Demons are often in view when Jesus redresses suffering by a word of command. The demons irresistibly obeyed, as did the weather, fevers, and loaves of bread. Yet the ekballistic confrontations between Jesus and the spirits do not have the feel of titanic combat between forces of moral good and immoral evil. Instead, they have the feel of a compassionate alleviation of human misery. The reason is that EMM and other power modes redressed situational evils, not moral evil. EMM is not really about "spiritual warfare."

On the other hand, the gospels narrate one long "truth encounter" between Jesus and the moral evil that contends for or fills the human heart. The titanic moral combat occurs in the classic spiritual-warfare mode—Jesus' temptations in the desert and in the garden of Gethsemane—as the Son learned obedience through what he suffered. Throughout his ministry, Jesus rescued those in moral bondage to Satan by words of truth that claimed authority over temptation, sin, and unbelief. Inhabiting spirits are never in view. The real spiritual *warfare* engages moral, not situational, evil. The great physician may give medicine to bring down blood pressure—EMM temporarily alleviating situational evil. But he challenges the patient to quit smoking, drinking, and gorging on junk food—moral evil. The latter is the decisive battlefield.

Consider an example of the continual interplay between modes as situational and moral evil alternate on the stage of Scripture. Mark 7–8 offers a compact, typical case study. The Pharisees teach falsehoods, so Jesus reproves them and teaches about the iniquity of the human heart (moral; 7:1–23). A little girl suffers demonization, which is compared metaphorically to needing food, so Jesus drives out the demon (situational; 7:24–30). A deaf and partially dumb man is brought to Jesus, so Jesus heals him (situational; 7:31–37). The crowds are hungry, so Jesus feeds them by a work of merciful power (situational; 8:1–9). The Pharisees' and disciples' hearts are hard, so Jesus reproves them (moral; 8:10–21). A blind man is brought to him, so Jesus heals him (situational; 8:22–26). Peter shows faith then unbelief, so Jesus charges, then reproves him as a Satan[9] (moral; 8:27–33). Jesus then teaches on the necessity of dying to one's self (moral; 8:34–38). Moral evil is no less Satanic than situational evil, but different problems obviously demand different sorts of solutions.[10]

WAS THERE A CHANGE OF METHODOLOGY?

There is certainly a change of methodology from the Old Testament to the gospels for dealing with *situational evil*, but we must not overdraw the contrast. The older way to fight situational evil typically involved prayer for God's deliverance and efforts to ameliorate suffering and injustice. Then Jesus came and used power encounters to create instant relief. But, obviously, the change in methodology between Testaments is not absolute. The New Testament often describes normal ways of addressing evil, such as the ways we are taught to pray and how Jesus gave money to the poor and confronted injustice. And the Old Testament, too, had seasons where divine power, through the prophets, overcame situational evil. Moses divided the Red Sea and Jordan River and provided manna and water in the desert; Elijah and Elisha brought a series of mercies and judgments.

But generally in the Old Testament people cried out to God for deliverance from afflictions, repenting when their sins were the proximate cause and pursuing justice and mercy. Some passages, such as Leviticus 26:14–39, 1 Kings 8, and Lamentations, present cases where situational evil is a just disciplinary consequence of moral evil, intended to bring about repentance and seeking refuge in the LORD. Other passages, such as Psalm 31, Psalm 44, and Isaiah 53, present cases where situational evil is unjust; they become occasions to seek refuge in the LORD and act with courage. Psalm 107 gives examples of both just and unjust suffering. Still other passages, such as Psalm 52 and Isaiah 24, present cases where situational evil is a just, final punitive consequence of moral evil. Whether the final result is situational good or situational evil, there is one common denominator: "Then they will know that I am the LORD."

In the New Testament, something extraordinary happened in the power encounters. God in the flesh answered the cry of misery himself immediately. The Shepherd himself bound up the wounds of his people. And people responded in amazement, "Who is *this* that wind and wave, demon and illness, bread and fish obey him?" We should *expect* that when the LORD himself arrived, natural evils would be demolished by power encounters.

We might expect that when the LORD arrived, *moral evils* would also be demolished by a power encounter: the fiery judgment on all wickedness. John the Baptist certainly expected a power encounter with moral evil, and thus the end of the need for classic spiritual warfare. Instead Jesus refused to call down fire on his opponents. The power encounter with moral evil happened when the Lamb obeyed unto death, bore the fiery wrath of justice, and was raised by the power of the Spirit to indestructible life. Satan can no longer hold the nations in darkness under the power of sin and death. Thus the strong man is being plundered as people from all nations come to the light.

There was never a change in the actual methodology for dealing with moral evil: pride, lust, anger, fear, lying, self-righteousness, drunkenness, unbelief, idolatry, occult practice, and all the other sins that inhabit human hearts and lives. Repeated sin puts people in moral bondage, but not in bondage to indwelling spirits. Satan's attempt to gain and sustain moral hegemony remains the core issue of spiritual warfare with the infallible mode being the classic mode. Again the conclusion is inescapable: EMM—which Jesus used to attack the consequences of sin— never became the mode of choice to attack sin, the cause.

Similarly, there was no change of methodology in dealing with moral evil that assails us from others. When we have been sinned against, even heinously, demons do not gain access or control. Abuse may produce incalculable anguish, tempting and teaching us to return profound evil for profound evil. But our response to moral evil remains a moral issue: Forgiveness or bitterness? Courage or fear? Truth or lies? Hope or despair? Love our enemies or hate and fear them? Return good or return evil? Renewal into the image of Christ or reinforcement in the image of Satan?

The classic mode of warfare—what it meant to seek and know God in a dark world—was taught in intricate detail in the Law and the Prophets, in Job, Psalms, and Proverbs. It was then reiterated in the whole New Testament. Yes, Jesus is the model for this mode of spiritual warfare. What Jesus did to fight spiritual warfare with moral evil is what we are to do: Trust in God's word of truth and obey through the indwelling power of the Holy Spirit.[11]

WRONG TOOLS, WRONG TASKS

EMM theology makes a serious misstep because it does not follow the Bible's clear distinction between sin and suffering. Because most EMM advocates do not look closely enough at texts in context, they tangle together sin and suffering, classic and ekballistic methods. The result is a confused, distorted, misleading practical theology that uses the wrong tools for the wrong tasks.

Moral evil is the overwhelming focus of contemporary EMM case studies. Case after case describes problems that Jesus would have treated in the classic, not the ekballistic, mode. The catalogue of "demons" in EMM literature and practice is in fact a catalogue of common sins: deep-rooted, compulsive patterns of anger, lust, occult practice, pride, fear, unbelief, and so forth. The "ground" by which demons supposedly gain access and sustain residency privileges is a moral ground; it is the sins just mentioned compounded by our own and others' past sins.

EMM advocates claim to follow the model of Jesus for spiritual warfare, but their model is actually more rooted in the occult worldview than the Bible's. They incorrectly take Jesus' model for fighting situational evil and adapt it to fighting moral evil. By demonizing sin, EMM theology actually embraces a worldview that the Bible opposes.

Here I am focusing on EMM distinctives, though in practice most EMM practitioners introduce elements of classic spiritual warfare that create an odd mixture of modes. The demonized are often held responsible to do classic spiritual warfare, yet also stand in need of EMM to treat moral bondages. It is as if Jesus told the rich young ruler to repent of mammon worship and follow him, but then cast out demons of Mammon and Self-righteousness that were hindering his repentance.

Neil Anderson's system illustrates the tension. He takes a long and constructive step away from EMM when he teaches that a "truth encounter" should replace a "power encounter." Instead of conversing with demons, Anderson talks to people, inviting them to faith in core evangelical doctrines of God's grace and our new identity in Christ. But he still conceptualizes the underlying problem as resident demons of sin. So what Anderson does in effect is teach people to drive out their own sin demons by using the modes of classic spiritual warfare. His system is therefore a hybrid. He misdefines the problem—retaining the

EMM model of sin as indwelling demons—but supplies the right solution.

The problems of the EMM approach are practical as well as theoretical. EMM's demonization of sin generates a defective mode of pastoral care and counsel, a defective mode of self-counsel, a defective mode of spiritual warfare. True spiritual warfare is being obscured by current versions of ekballistic ministry that bear little resemblance to Jesus' practice and purposes in casting out demons and even less resemblance to what Scripture teaches about our daily warfare. Granted, EMM techniques typically do not replace the classic mode entirely, but supplement it. But the EMM worldview, with its notion of inhabiting demon lords, perverts the biblical worldview. Although the more sober EMM practitioners attempt to downplay the importance of casting out demons, the demonological worldview has a large and mischievous influence that their cautions cannot prevent. It does make people think that Satan's connection to our inward battles with sin is a matter of spirit inhabitation. The phrase "spiritual problem" tends to be defined as an "indwelling spirit" problem.

 We have addressed the continuity between Jesus' mode of ministry and ours—the classic mode of spiritual warfare. But we have not addressed possible discontinuities between us and Jesus. Jesus often acted in ways that we are not called to imitate. In the next chapter we will examine the numerous shifts in the mode of ministry found in Scripture.

6

JESUS' MODE OF MINISTRY AND OURS

THE EKBALLISTIC MODE OF REDRESSING SUFFERING does not stand alone among Jesus' mighty works of compassion and self-revelation. He performed many dramatic signs of power: he cast out demons, healed the sick, raised the dead and was raised himself, walked on the water, multiplied loaves and fish, and so forth. There are some obvious discontinuities between what Jesus did and what we are to do; there are also continuities. Scripture teaches us to discern the difference.

In this chapter we will look at eleven examples of Jesus' works that we are called to do in a fashion different from our master. Notice three things about each example. First, Jesus addresses genuine human needs that continue today. Second, Jesus performs a particular action in an unusually striking and authoritative way, a command-control mode: "I say it. It happens." Third, we are told—by precept or example—to accomplish the same work but in a different way, the classic faith-obedience mode. The mode shifts. There are good biblical reasons to believe that ekballistic healing from demons has been replaced by the classic mode.

Before we start it is important to note that mode shifts are not unique to the New Testament. The Old Testament gives a striking example of a mode shift in regard to feeding people. When the Israelites wandered in the desert the LORD miraculously provided for their daily needs—the manna appeared each morning and water flowed from the rock. But the moment the

Israelites crossed the Jordan, things changed. They ate the last of the manna when they entered the land of milk and honey, fields and fruit trees, springs of running water. A power encounter with natural evil had reversed the curse of the parched desert for forty years, but then the people became farmers and herdsmen. The immediate power mode always served to accomplish particular divine purposes. In the Sinai desert it tested—and, for a few people, taught—daily dependency, fidelity, gratitude, and hope. The spiritual warfare in Sinai was moral, only occasioned by the parched desert and God's mode of providing their physical needs.

These eleven examples that follow build in a rough order, ending with those closest to EMM. Some examples speak of what might seem for some to be relatively minor parts of life: fishing, the weather, taxes. Other examples seem relatively more weighty: forgiving sins, healing the sick, raising the dead. But a consistent pattern will emerge.

1. PAY TAXES

Jesus and the apostle Peter paid their taxes in an unusual way—at least once. Jesus sent Peter fishing with instructions that the payment for their temple tax would be found in the mouth of the first fish Peter caught.[1] In this instance the command-control mode served an explicit teaching purpose. The LORD himself need not pay taxes in his own temple; yet, in order not to give offense, he paid the tax in a way that revealed who he was.

Other Scriptures explicitly command us to pay our taxes, assuming we will use more normal methods.[2] The need to pay taxes abides but the mode of raising the money changes. Of course, we are never forbidden to use windfall money to pay our taxes. But Jesus' command-control mode, which created a windfall, is clearly superseded—as it was preceded—by the classic stewardship mode. Work, and pay what is owed.

Notice that the idea of a mode shift between what Jesus does and what we are to do is not really an argument from silence. Scripture gives us no command not to control nature by a word of power in order to get tax money. But because the rest of Scripture teaches and exemplifies a different mode, such a prohibition would be absurd and redundant.

2. CATCH FISH

On two other occasions Jesus also used the authoritative command mode to direct the apostles' fishing trips.[3] These were power encounters with situational evil: in both cases, the fishermen had worked all night but caught nothing. Jesus used his power to bless his afflicted people, rolling back the curse of futile labor. In both cases, Jesus' command resulted in a staggering catch. The recognition that only the LORD had such power brought varied reactions. Peter was humbled in the first case: "Go away from me, Lord; I am a sinful man." In the second case he jumped into the water in joyful recognition.

In both cases Jesus' mode had a pointed purpose. With fishing, as with paying taxes, Jesus commanded his apostles to do something that revealed his control over the natural world. Are we to follow his mode? Here we have no direct command, only the example of the apostles. When Jesus was not physically present, they fished as they always had. As with the example of the tax money in the fish's mouth—but different from casting out demons and healing—the apostles fished in the power-encounter mode only as the audience and beneficiaries of Jesus' direct command.

3. WALK ON WATER

The gospels record that Jesus and Peter both walked on the surface of the Sea of Galilee.[4] Jesus walked on water because he was the creator of heaven and earth, the maker of water. And Peter walked on water through faith in Jesus as he responded to Christ's command. But Peter began to sink when he lost faith. Jesus rescued and then rebuked him. Jesus used this enacted parable as a living demonstration of the nature of faith. The power encounter also compelled faith directly: "Then those who were in the boat worshiped him, saying, 'Truly you are the Son of God.'"

Today—and throughout the Bible—similar issues of faith are ever present. But now we normally express faith by walking through the deep waters rather than walking on the water. The mode of expressing faith has shifted to the classic mode.

4. FEED THE HUNGRY, GIVE DRINK TO THE THIRSTY

Hunger and thirst—and their many causes—are abiding situational evils. Drought, thorns, locusts, social injustice, enemy invasion, and laziness all can lead to deprivation and even death. The LORD God as a judge made himself known by bringing these evils on those who turned away from him. The LORD God as a savior made himself known by providing for those who took refuge in him. Sometimes he used power encounters: the manna, the quail, Elijah's ravens, the poor widow's bowl of flour and jar of oil. Sometimes he used more "normal" demonstrations of sovereign power: the land flowing with milk and honey, Joseph's prominence in Egypt, the timing of drought and rainfall.

On two occasions Jesus' mode of redressing this evil was to pray and then multiply small amounts of food in order to feed vast crowds. And once he turned water into wine to bless a celebration. Jesus used this mode to accomplish three things: Reveal himself as the LORD, do people tangible good, and invite faith. The miraculous wine at Cana, for example, invited witnesses to ponder Psalm 104:15: The LORD God brings forth "wine that gladdens the heart of man." Jesus displayed his divine power dramatically.

John 6 offers the lengthiest discussion of the purposes of the power-encounter mode. Giving money to the poor could also feed hungry people, a mode that Jesus evidently used routinely.[5] But feeding the hungry on command was an act of love in itself, temporarily sustaining life. And the miracle also provided an opportunity to teach about more profound human needs. The bread that sustained temporal life for a day pointed to the true bread that would sustain life eternally.

What Jesus did in feeding the five thousand typifies other instances. The command-control mode attracted a great deal of attention, revealing that Jesus was at least a prophet of the LORD—another Moses, Elijah, or Elisha—and was perhaps the LORD himself. As God had given manna to the Israelites in the desert, so now the people ate extraordinary bread. But the mode was not an end in itself, meant to be perpetuated. The mode of Jesus' assaults on situational evil always had the triple focus of being genuine acts of love to needy people, revealing that he was God and Christ incarnate, and prompting faith that people might believe.

We also must feed hungry people, and our mode follows Jesus' example up to a point: we, too, pray. But the Bible teaches a fundamental discontinuity of mode between what Jesus did next and what we do. When we pray the Lord's Prayer, "give us this day our daily bread," we ask God to provide. We either eat the fruit that our own work provides or we eat what others share with us in love. Where Jesus multiplied loaves and fishes, we give to the church, support relief organizations, organize a food cupboard, nurse infants, make supper for our children, show hospitality.

Why do we not use supernatural means to feed the hungry today? Is it simply that we know that by ourselves we cannot? We have no command not to multiply loaves and fishes, but Scripture elsewhere tells us to do something different by both command and example. Paul, for instance, worked diligently to meet his own needs and help the needy.[6] Ephesians 4:28 tells us to work with our hands so that we can share with those in need. Paul wrote at length to the Corinthians to raise money to help a church in a famine region. The pastoral mode replaced the power-encounter mode.

5. SPEAK WITH GOD'S AUTHORITY

How do humans express God's authority? Jesus spoke with direct, personal authority, saying, "I say to you." He did not speak "as the scribes or the Pharisees" or as we speak. Although we have authority—God's authority—we do not speak in the same way Jesus did. Our authority fundamentally says, "The Bible says. . ." "The Lord says. . ." "God says. . . ." This is not weak or impersonal; a sense of gravity and urgency can fill our words: "In the name of the Lord, I solemnly charge you, I plead with you. . . ." The Lord's authority can even be unstated rather than overt: "You are killing yourself by what you believe and how you live. Repent or you will die."[7] In any case, ours is a derivative authority, not our own. Our authority is a signpost pointing to the one with all authority in heaven and on earth. Jesus spoke with first-person authority, but we dare not talk that way or else we sin.

6. CALL PEOPLE TO MINISTRY

How did Jesus call people to ministry? He spotted a disciple-to-be and said, "Leave your tax table, leave your nets, come with me." Jesus spoke; the apostles obeyed. Later, Jesus' power encounter with Saul blinded him and knocked him to the ground: "Now get up and go into the city, and you will be told what you must do" (Acts 9:6). Jesus used the command-control mode with unopposable authority.

We, too, must call people and hear the call to ministry. We do not use the command-control mode, but look to Scripture's guidelines in such passages as 1 Timothy 3. Scripture gives objective criteria: character, willingness, experience, reputation, and gifts. We test people, watching their lives over time; we pray to our Lord for wisdom.

In many of these eleven examples Jesus used both modes, which is appropriate for the God-man. He first called his disciples in a dramatic and striking way; he then prayed all night before finally selecting twelve to be apostles. Similarly, he ate food that was grown and prepared normally. He crossed the lake in a boat. He quoted Scripture. He used money that had been acquired and donated in normal ways. Even in Jesus' life the command-control mode had a distinct purpose and limited place. The Bible is silent in the sense that it never says *not* to use authoritative commands to call leaders; it is a loud silence, however, because we are given so many instructions about how to use the classic mode.

7. FORGIVE SINS

There are striking continuities and discontinuities between Jesus and us when it comes to dealing with sins. The continuity is at the point of need: there are always people to be forgiven. But Jesus deals with the sins of others quite differently than we do. He provides a substitutionary atonement; he actually and objectively forgives them by acting as the perfect sacrifice on their behalf. He can say, "Father, forgive them" with authority because he speaks as the one who earned the right to forgive people by shedding his own blood for them.

Interestingly, the Gospel of John mentions only one case of ekballistic ministry: "Now the ruler of this world shall be cast out. And I, if I be lifted up from the earth, will draw all men to myself" (John 12:31–32, NASB). The ultimate exorcism takes place on the cross, where Satan's power to hold us in bondage to sin and death was destroyed. John's lone case of "EMM" delivers the mortal wound to the power and penalty of moral evil.

The discontinuity between Jesus' mode and ours is that we do not die for sin—our own or other people's; we do not create the objective conditions of forgiveness. But the point of continuity is that as recipients of deliverance from the kingdom of darkness, we forgive people as God has forgiven us. We forgive others as *recipients* of Jesus' mode of forgiving: "Forgive each other, just as God in Christ also has forgiven you" (Ephesians 4:32, NASB). Our mode is different not only in the ground of forgiveness, but the process. We can forgive another's sins against us, but we do not forgive the same way God forgives. If a person asks for our forgiveness and is a hypocrite, we still forgive subjectively, holding no grudge against him or her. But the hypocrite will remain unforgiven objectively, because God reads the heart. Jesus does authoritative, objective forgiving; we do personal, subjective forgiving.

8. CONFRONT AND CURSE SIN

The other side of dealing with sin also exemplifies the mode shift. Jesus Christ and the apostles brought wrath to bear immediately. For example Jesus said to the fig tree, "May you never bear fruit again!" The tree—a picture of unfruitful Israel—withered and died instantly. Peter named the sins of Ananias and Sapphira, who immediately dropped dead. This power encounter deals with moral evil by bringing forward situational evil as an immediate consequence. Imagine that kind of authority operating in a church stewardship campaign today. The pastor could see into the hearts of people. To anyone who fudged a little in order to look good he would simply say, "You're lying and deceiving the Holy Spirit" and would then call the undertaker. But obviously this does not happen because the church is not called to express the just wrath of God in the same way Jesus did.

The need to bring judgment abides. But the Lord and his prophets and apostles command us to exert authority through "normal" means: preaching the word of God, carrying out church discipline, defending the rights of the oppressed, confronting and warning evildoers. Jesus speaks directly and on his own authority; our authority is derivative and qualified. When Jesus declared divine curses in Matthew 23 he offered no grace; we need to offer grace, the opportunity for repentance and forgiveness.[8]

9. RAISE THE DEAD

Raising the dead is the supreme attack on situational evil, for death is the ultimate logic of all other evils. Jesus raised the dead through both the extraordinary, command-control mode and the normal, dependent-faith mode. In his warfare of compassion against the ultimate situational evil he commanded, "Young man, I say to you, get up!" and "My child, get up!" and "Lazarus, come out!"[9] But in facing his own moral call to an obedience unto death, he believed, "The Son of Man must . . . be raised up on the third day" (Luke 9:22, NASB) and entrusted himself to him who judges righteously.

How do we raise the dead? We use the second mode, saying, "Believe in the Lord Jesus Christ, who is the resurrection and the life. If you believe in him, you will live even if you die. And if you live and believe in him you shall never die." Similarly we entrust our souls to a faithful creator. Jesus raised the young man of Nain, Jairus' daughter, and Lazarus, but we presume they later died. But Jesus himself was raised as the firstfruits of the better resurrection of all who love him.

Jesus' three power encounters with death provided tokens of love and signs of divine power that were stunning but temporary. But his central mode of raising the dead through dependent faith in a word of truth works better and lasts longer. Jesus' rarer mode is breathtaking, but it is not finally as powerful as the "normal" mode by which he operates in his universe. This is partly why Jesus says, "I tell you the truth, anyone who has faith in me will do what I have been doing. He will do even greater things than these, because I am going to the Father" (John 14:12). Not surprisingly, Jesus then speaks in great detail about prayer, love, and the Holy Spirit. We have received ways of living through the Spirit's power that are more powerful, if sometimes less dramatic, than the command-control mode. When Jesus was on earth, God's glory depended on his immediate authoritative presence. But we are given a mode that can reach throughout the world. We are to raise all who believe in Christ through the preaching of his gospel.

10. CONTROL THE WEATHER

Our final two examples—controlling the weather and healing sickness—are the most pointed because the Bible closely links them to ekballistic ministry. As modern people we may not care about the weather except as an inconvenience; we rarely depend on it directly. But we ought to care, because it affects human life and God says repeatedly that he controls it.[10] When I spent time in Uganda a number of years ago it seemed so strange to me—a suburban American—when our pastor prayed fervently for the rains to come. He had the right idea; I had to grow up to know the God of power.

Jesus, as the LORD God, performed a power encounter with situational evil in dealing with the weather. The specific incident occurred after a notably long day of teaching. Jesus was sleeping in the boat when a fierce storm struck. The boat was foundering before the fearful disciples woke him. Jesus spoke to the wind and waves, "Quiet! Be still!" His command stilled the storm immediately.[11]

We learn our mode of dealing with weather through the many passages that portray God in control of meteorological events and exhibit God's people praying to him. For example, even "Give us this day our daily bread" entails prayers to God regarding the weather. Hardships, whether deserved or undeserved, prompt intercession. The prophet Elijah offers a fascinating example of someone who operated in both the command-control mode and the dependent prayer mode. As an agent of God's judgment, he proclaims, "There will be neither dew nor rain in the next few years except at my word" (1 Kings 17:1). And yet finally the rain, like the fire, fell in answer to his prayers.[12] Interestingly, in commanding us how to help sufferers, James 5:17–18 draws an analogy between the weather and sickness, commending to us only Elijah's prayer life for our emulation.

Jesus in the swamping boat operated in the command mode; we operate in the mode of dependent request, asking our Father to work in power. One is not more effective than the other. They are different, but have equally strong effects. For instance, Elijah prayed and there was no rain for three years. He prayed again and the storm came that day. The Ugandan pastor prayed, the seasonal rains arrived several days later. This is God's world.

A comparison of Mark 4:35–41 with Mark 1:23–28 demonstrates how Jesus' power over the weather explicitly connects with his power over demons. Mark 1:23–27 describes Jesus' first power encounter: "Just then a man in their synagogue who was possessed by an evil spirit cried out, 'What do you want with us, Jesus of Nazareth? Have you come to destroy us? I know who you are—the Holy One of God!' 'Be quiet!' said Jesus sternly. 'Come out of him!' The evil spirit shook the man violently and came out of him with a shriek. The people were all so amazed that they asked each other, 'What is this? A new teaching—and with authority! He even gives orders to evil spirits and they obey him.' "

Compare this passage to Mark 4:38–41, when Jesus calmed the storm. "Jesus was in the stern, sleeping on a cushion. The disciples woke him and said to him, 'Teacher, don't you care if we drown?' He got up, rebuked the wind and said to the waves, 'Quiet! Be still!' Then the wind died down and it was completely calm. He said to his disciples, 'Why are you so afraid? Do you still have no faith?' They were terrified and asked each other, 'Who is this? Even the wind and the waves obey him!' "

The passages are virtually identical thematically and verbally—only the details differ. We can draw at least seven direct parallels. First, both situational evils stormed noisily at Jesus in ways appropriate to a spirit and a gale. Second, Jesus spoke direct rebukes and commands to them. Third, Jesus commanded the same thing in both cases: "Be quiet!" Fourth, both the demon and the storm instantly obeyed: the demon left the man; the wind died down. Fifth, witnesses were stunned, amazed, and afraid, which is the typical response to Jesus' use of the command-control mode. Sixth, in the people's amazement they wondered, "What is this authority? Who is this man?" And seventh, the witnesses commented on what they saw: situational evils—unclean spirits, wind and sea—doing exactly what Jesus told them to do.

The disciples marveled, "Who is this man?" because they knew the Scriptures. Psalm 107:29 says, "[The LORD] stilled the storm to a whisper; the waves of the sea were hushed." And the crowds marveled at Jesus' authority over evil spirits because they knew the Scriptures. As we saw throughout the Old Testament, the LORD's permission and will control the evil spirits.

Thus the command-control mode deals identically with the weather and unclean spirits, two forms of situational evil. They are in the same category: harmful, destructive expressions of the curse.[13] Jesus' mode brought the first taste and glimpse of deliverance from all forms of suffering. The final power encounter with situational evil will come when Jesus returns in glory.

As with the other examples, we see a mode shift for dealing with weather. Jesus speaks, the weather obeys. But we pray to God for deliverance from the sufferings produced by bad weather.

11. HEAL THE SICK

Our final example is the most significant for evaluating EMM. Healing the sick and casting out demons are repeatedly placed in the same category to the extent that Scripture frequently says that Jesus heals people of demons.[14] Sickness is a great evil, a foretaste of death. Jesus heals the sick by speaking a word. Then the blind see, the deaf hear, the lame walk, the fevered cool off, the withered regain strength.

Jesus was moved by compassion to alleviate physical suffering. He brought both relief and joy to the afflicted. These good works are repeatedly spoken of as signs of Jesus' identity, the one who "heals all your diseases, who redeems your life from the pit," who "bind[s] up the brokenhearted [and] comfort[s] all who mourn."[15]

Healings—both before and after they occurred—were repeatedly linked to Jesus' call to place faith in him as healer. On several occasions Jesus also explicitly used healing power to establish his authority to forgive sins. As often is the case, the Gospel of John throws the most extensive light on the wider purposes of Jesus' mode. In John 9 Jesus healed the blind man to reveal the works of God, invite faith, and drive unbelief into the open. In John 11 Jesus raised Lazarus to teach a bigger lesson:

"I am the resurrection and the life." The command-control mode compelled faith; it also hardened unbelief into murderous intent.

Should we also use the command-control mode to heal? Scripture explicitly instructs us otherwise. The normal mode of healing in both the Old and New Testaments is to pray, placing primary reliance on God, and then to employ medical means. Prayerful faith in God the healer lays the foundation. Perhaps the best illustration of the classic mode of healing occurs in Isaiah 38. King Hezekiah is near death from an infection, and prays with great anguish of heart to God for deliverance from his affliction. God hears him. Medical treatment—applying a poultice to the boil—follows (Isaiah 38:21), but putting God first is crucial. Another king's suffering warns against forgetting to put first things first. Asa became severely diseased in his feet, "but even in his illness he did not seek help from the LORD, but only from the physicians. Then . . . Asa died and rested with his fathers" (2 Chronicles 16:12–13).

Some will respond that it is an argument from silence to say that we do not heal using Jesus' command-control mode. After all, they point out, there is no command not to heal using Jesus' mode just as there is no negative command for any of the previous ten examples. But Scripture specifically tells us to approach sickness a different way. James 5:14–16 teaches the church what methodology to use. "Is any one of you sick? He should call the elders of the church to pray over him and anoint him with oil in the name of the Lord. And the prayer offered in faith will make the sick person well; the Lord will raise him up. If he has sinned, he will be forgiven. Therefore confess your sins to each other and pray for each other so that you may be healed. The prayer of a righteous man is powerful and effective."

Four points stand out in this passage about how we should ask God to work powerfully on behalf of sick people. First, the shepherds of the church should get involved in a personal way. General prayers from the pulpit are not sufficient; prayer for the sick is hands-on, face-to-face work.

Second, sickness often creates a counseling context, so confession of sins is mentioned. Situational evils, sickness included, frequently bring varied sins to the surface. Sickness may be a judgment on sin, either as a natural consequence or a specific punishment. Or it may occasion temptations to sin: fears, despair, self-pity, selfishness, anger, escapism, regret, grumbling, trusting medicine, trusting faith healers, denying reality, and so forth. Or sickness may prompt self-examination that brings awareness of previously unseen sins. Sickness creates tremendous counseling opportunities to minister the grace of Christ and to help people grow in faith and obedience.

Third, Scripture never despises the use of medical means. James 5 may directly encourage the use of medical means when it speaks of "anointing him with oil in the name of the Lord." In English this sounds like a ceremonial anointing. But the word James uses for "anoint" is not the word typically used for spiritual or ceremonial anointing. The word used usually describes rubbing in ointments medicinally or using oils to cleanse and groom the human body. Oils were the basis of the most common medical treatments. If this is James's intent, then his exhortation is to employ medical means as an act of faith in God. "In the name of the Lord" stresses that medical treatment must not be received as an act of faith in medicine but as an act of faith in the Lord who heals.

Fourth, James 5 encourages robust prayer by giving the example of Elijah. The prayer mode calls on the same power—God's—that the command-control mode also expressed. Jesus did healings one way; the Bible tells us to do them another way.

A MODE SWITCH FOR DEMONIC AFFLICTIONS?

Matthew, Mark, Luke, and Acts portray Jesus and the apostles using the command-control mode to address sickness, the weather, paying taxes, speaking with personal authority, and so forth. The rest of the New Testament, following the main approach in the Old Testament, exemplifies and commands a different mode. Is there a similar mode switch for dealing with demons associated with ailments and afflictions?

We certainly will not be surprised to find a mode shift. Scripture is "silent" on the issue in the same way it is silent on paying taxes, performing resurrections, or stilling storms by words of command. The silence thunders. The mode of addressing demonically induced sufferings reverts to the classic mode: Live the Christian life of receptive faith and active obedience in the midst of life's hardships. We will explore this shift in the course of the next two chapters.

EMM, similar to every other example, served temporary purposes. Scripture gives no command to perpetuate EMM. Similarly, the epistles consistently evidence the classic-mode approach to demonic (and other) sufferings, analogous to the Old Testament. But it is worth noting that Scripture does not abound with examples of demonic suffering, outside of the examples from the Old Testament and the gospels already discussed. Most of the Bible's attention is directed to the true spiritual warfare with the powers of sin, something that never involved EMM in the gospels or anywhere else.

The modern demon-deliverance ministries are predicated on two fundamental errors. First, they misread the biblical record and fail to distinguish between moral evil and situational evil. They cast out "demons" of moral evil, something neither taught nor illustrated anywhere in Scripture. Second, they fail to reckon with the general mode shift away from the command-control mode and toward the classic mode.

There are serious theological and pastoral consequences of going beyond Scripture. If we are to address one situational evil—spirits that cause affliction—differently from how we address every other situational evil, we will need good reasons and clear instructions. And if we are to widen the use of the EMM mode dramatically—supposing that spirits infiltrate the human personality, take up residence, and secretly exacerbate and constrain patterns of sin and unbelief—we will need utterly compelling reasons.

EMM advocates are not following Jesus' model when they link demonization with sin patterns. Jesus never does this. In effect, they advocate their own radical mode switch—a new use for EMM as a necessary supplement to Jesus' classic mode—with neither direct biblical warrant nor any analogy from Scripture. Neither the Old Testament nor Jesus nor the letters in the New Testament say that EMM addresses the moral dilemma of our hearts, our bondage to sin, or our warfare with Satan as a would-be lord. The way of progressive sanctification in the face of life's troubles is a different way.

A HOST OF
FURTHER QUESTIONS

THE ARGUMENT OF THE LAST CHAPTER—that there is a change in mode away from the almost unique ekballistic ministry of Jesus—provokes many further questions. Why did Jesus use the extraordinary mode? Is the ekballistic mode passé, like manna from heaven? If so, what do we do when we meet someone with a background in the occult? What do we do when we encounter profound, even uncanny, moral evil that creates bondage on the inside of a person's life? This chapter will tackle these questions.

WHY DID JESUS CAST OUT DEMONS?

At a fundamental level Jesus did good to demonized people. The boy whom the demon convulsed found relief. The man driven mad with restless torment was observed sitting down, clothed, and in his right mind. The woman bent over double stood up straight. The woman's daughter who had been cruelly demonized found healing. The man who had been blinded and silenced became able to speak and see. Jesus revealed that he is the one whom the evil spirits must obey; that he is the LORD, the Holy One of God, the Son of God.

But the ekballistic mode not only did good, it revealed Jesus' identity and sparked brisk debate between faith and unbelief. Some believed and rejoiced. Others hardened their hearts, blasphemed the power of the Holy Spirit, and accused Jesus of being in league with the devil.

Thus Jesus' power encounters—with hunger, sickness, death, and demonic suffering—are enacted parables. They gave an experience of heaven so that people might repent of their sins and believe in the Savior. Jesus used a mode suited to awaken faith so that he might bind the strong man and plunder the kingdom of sin. The fulfillment of the power-encounter mode will come when Christ returns to usher in the kingdom of heaven.

This explains why there are no commands or instructions in Scripture for us to do EMM. Consider the sweep of the Gospel of Luke, for example. Luke alternates among historical narratives, the mighty works of Jesus, and the words of Jesus. Throughout the book, Jesus travels, does works of power, and teaches. One might assume that Jesus would teach about how to do the command-control works he did, but not so. Every miracle teaches about who Jesus is, arouses faith, or provokes controversy. But when Jesus teaches, he teaches about the classic mode of the Christian life and spiritual warfare: repentance, faith, commitment to him, how to love, the use of the tongue, alertness, reconciliation, integrity, identifying false teachers, how to handle money, prayer, and so on.

Jesus says nothing about how to do power works. Nothing about demons of sin. Nothing about casting out demons from oneself as the way to solve personal problems and grow as a believer. Nothing about delivering new converts by something more deep hitting than repentance and faith. Instead, Jesus taught on the same sorts of issues previously taught in the Old Testament and subsequently taught in the epistles. If EMM was to be a continuing strategy, it would surely follow that we would be instructed on whether and how to do it.

Read Matthew, Mark, Luke, and Acts with this perspective in mind. Notice how consistently Scripture includes statements and stories that reveal the *purpose* of the command-control mode. With virtually every miracle, we are told or shown the purpose; we are not told to do likewise. For example, John the

Baptist sent messengers asking, "Are you the One who was to come, or should we expect someone else?" At that very hour Jesus set off a fireworks show of command-control works to bless the afflicted (Luke 7:18–23).[1] The deliverance mode served to attest, declare, accredit, bear witness, and confirm.

The mode also identified Jesus' authoritative messengers in the establishment of the church: "Everyone was filled with awe, and many wonders and miraculous signs were done by the apostles" (Acts 2:43).[2] The purpose of the mode in all of these passages is to attest to the identity and authority of the one bringing the message.

No Commands for EMM

There is no direct command in Scripture to do EMM, even to relieve suffering. And—to repeat—contrary to EMM teaching, moral evil is not in view either in demonization or ekballistics. But what about demonic torments that need healing? Is there reason to expect a mode shift to the classic way of facing and addressing situational evil? Do any passages from Scripture give *possible* warrant for an ongoing ekballistic method for relieving demon-induced sufferings?

Mark 16:17–18 comes closest to giving us a clear expectation that EMM will continue: "And these signs will accompany those who believe: In my name they will drive out demons; they will speak in new tongues; they will pick up snakes with their hands; and when they drink deadly poison, it will not hurt them at all; they will place their hands on sick people, and they will get well." In conversations with friends who advocate EMM, this passage was the only one cited as a positive command. Most EMM books simply assume that EMM continues. Their argument is usually: "If the devil and demons are nonfactors, we wouldn't need to cast out demons. If the devil and demons are still factors, we'll need to cast out demons." They fail to consider that the devil and demons could still be a factor but that EMM would not be the mode to use.

At best the meaning of Mark 16 is ambiguous regarding our use of ekballistic methods. It could be read as if these various signs will accompany *everyone* who believes the message of the apostles. In this case, we would expect to do ekballistic work to bring healing from spirit-caused afflictions. Again, note that the biblical definition of the scope and purposes of ekballistics is a far cry from contemporary EMM theory and practice.

This passage, however, can also be interpreted to mean that the signs will accompany the apostles as they proclaim that Jesus is Lord. There are strong contextual reasons to favor this latter interpretation. The apostles' faith and unbelief is in view throughout 16:9–20. And in 16:20 the apostles did go forth and have their message confirmed by the signs that followed. Thus with the apostles in view, Mark 16:17 simply fits within the notion that there has been a general shift in the mode from Jesus and the apostles. Ekballistic encounters proved that Jesus is the Christ and that the apostles were Christ's representatives. There is no compelling reason to say that Mark 16:17 assumes we should do what the apostles did. Sound Bible interpretation understands more ambiguous passages in the light of clearer passages instead of building major teaching on uncertain passages.

Besides this passage's ambiguity and the fact that, on the more likely interpretation, it is consistent with the mode shift, Mark 16:17 has other features that are troubling to an EMM interpretation. We must take this passage as a whole rather than selecting bits we favor. But then what about the so-called charismatic issues: tongues and command-control healings? Many leading EMM advocates are anti-charismatic, and one leader even says that tongues are demonic deceits, and that tongue spirits must be cast out.[3] Therefore non-charismatic EMM advocates certainly can not use Mark 16 to make their case.

For both charismatics and non-charismatics, what about serpents and deadly poisons? We know that the Apostle Paul was bitten by a poisonous viper without harm (Act 28:3–6); this sign then acted a spur to proclaiming the gospel on Malta. This is consistent with the mode shift from the apostles' day to our own.

But groups that handle snakes today are almost universal deemed cultic or semicultic. Further, the reference to deadly poison is a complete mystery. Some people have tried this over the centuries: they died.

Mark 16:17 gives rise to one final problem. There is doubt as to whether this is even a valid part of Scripture, as most of the oldest Greek manuscripts do not contain 16:9–20. Perhaps these verses are genuine, perhaps they are not. Many Bible translations put it in brackets or have a footnote; some do not even include it. Therefore for many reasons Mark 16:17 is not a strong passage on which to build a case for ongoing ekballistic healing.

This ambiguous passage in Mark comes closest to commanding an abiding practice of ekballistic healing. Five other passages in the gospels and Acts describe the ekballistic practices of Jesus' disciples and others, but never tell us to do likewise. The teaching point of these passages, which are described briefly below, invariably moves in a different direction that often explicitly deemphasizes ekballistics.

First, Matthew 7:20–23 mentions the ekballistic activities of the damned as something that distracted them from the moral issues and the classic mode that Jesus had taught in the Sermon on the Mount. Second, Mark 9:38–40 describes a nondisciple who cast out demons, which Jesus used as an occasion to reprove the disciples' pride and encourage people to deal with their sins. Third and fourth, Luke 9:1–6 describes the apostles' ekballistic healings and 10:1–24 describes healings performed by the seventy-two sent out by Jesus. Both passages are consistent with the purposes of the command-control mode: spectacular, temporary relief from suffering; a revelation that Christ the king was present; spurs to faith; an object lesson for the coming blessings of the kingdom to all who repent and believe. In the latter passage Jesus makes a point to shift the disciple's attention away from the dramatics of ekballistic healing. Fifth, Acts 8:5–13 describes the ekballistic healings of the deacon Philip. The larger point of the passage is that such works signaled the spread of the gospel to the nations.

There are two points to make in summary. The first is that Scripture loudly rejects applying ekballistic methods to include our warfare with sin. The gospels are entirely consistent with both the Old Testament and the epistles. What should properly be called spiritual warfare is always conducted in the classic mode. EMM advocates, in contrast, have radically redefined the purposes of demon deliverance—redefining human nature, God, and the devil along the way—without biblical warrant. The second point is that the Bible neither gives us a direct command to do ekballistic healing nor teaches us how to do it such that we should presume it is an abiding activity. The consistent and cumulative silence of Scripture about ekballistic healing ought to give advocates serious pause.

If the church grasps the first point, much confusion will disappear. The vast majority of cases mislabeled "demonization" and mistreated with EMM will be seen for what they really are. People will be truly equipped to fight spiritual warfare with energy and intelligence. And if the church grasps the second point, the small remnant of cases that remain will similarly be treated with the energy and intelligence that should mark our efforts on behalf of the sick and suffering.

WHAT ABOUT OCCULT INVOLVEMENT?

EMM teachers emphasize various causes of demonic moral bondage, which they believe warrant EMM. Commonly cited sources of demons include occult or Satanic practices, whether dabbling in the occult, owning cultic artifacts, or making a full-fledged commitment to Satanism; deep-seated, habitual sins; the sins or occult practice of ancestors; experiences of severe victimization, such as sexual or Satanic ritual abuse. In the typical EMM view, moral evil, done or experienced, allows demonic agents to slip into crevices of the human personality.

Demonization is virtually assumed in someone with an occult or Satan-worshiping past. EMM is used to clear out residual demonic "strongholds" that continue to hold a person in greater or lesser bondage to unbelief, sins, blasphemous thoughts, and so forth. Occult practice would seem to be the strong case both for a moral-evil view of demonization and for the importance of an ekballistic methodology for sanctification.

The Bible addresses this issue in numerous places. In chapter 4 we indicated some of the teachings and implications of the Old Testament regarding people from an occult background. And the New Testament says a great deal about the occult—how to view it and minister to people involved in it. Several passages in Acts have striking implications for whether EMM should be used to help a person coming from an occult past. Acts 8 is probably the most striking. It tells of the "Samaritan Pentecost" as the gospel first spread from Jerusalem outward to the nations.[4] Along the way, Acts 8:5–24 tells of Simon the magician who was an occult practitioner of the highest order, manifesting astonishing power. But when Simon heard the gospel, he believed and was baptized. He had the typical reaction of amazement when he saw Philip casting out demons and healing. When Simon saw the power coming through Peter and John as they prayed for the Samaritans to receive the Holy Spirit, he wanted the same power. He even offered money for it.

What does this passage imply for someone coming from an occult past?[5] First, notice that Simon still operated in bondage to the occult mentality. He expressed a lust for spiritual power, or a lust to control power, for personal gain.[6] Simon was a professing believer, but sinful patterns of his occult past held him in bondage.

Second, notice that Acts 8 describes a setting where typical signs and wonders were being performed in Jesus' mode. Philip was casting out demons and healing, creating a tremendous stir (Acts 8:6–7, 13). If unclean spirits are slave-masters who inhabit the human heart to produce residual moral bondage in believers, we would expect Philip or the apostles to apply this method to Simon. If an ex-sorcerer, along with any convert out of an occult lifestyle, needs EMM done routinely, we would expect a dramatic vindication of the view that the occult leads to demon inhabitation and that effective ministry needs to bypass the human will to contact deeper, indwelling powers.

But third, notice Peter's response to Simon's request for power. Peter delivered one of the most stinging rebukes in all of Scripture, addressing Simon as a responsible moral being: "Your heart is not right before God. Repent of this wickedness and pray to the Lord. Perhaps he will forgive you for having such a thought in your heart" (Acts 8:21–22). Simon's heart was not right; it was *his* wickedness; *he* must repent and pray. Peter describes extreme bondage to sin and danger of damnation. Slavery to sin is a problem of the heart, not of aliens inhabiting the heart.

This passage undermines the presumption that occult involvement entails demonic inhabitation necessitating EMM. In fact we should remember that *most* converts to the Christian faith in the first century had occult, demon-worshiping, idolatrous backgrounds. The first Gentile converts turned from the outright dominion of Satan to God and were sanctified by faith in Jesus (Acts 26:18), not by EMM.

No doubt those involved in the occult have engaged in profound iniquity that may have lingering consequences. Residual patterns of evil—evil behaviors, false beliefs, self-serving motives, chaotic emotions, bizarre fantasies—may be strong. Temptations may arrive frequent and fierce, for Satan rages against his betrayers. Renewal of mind, purity of heart, and a lifestyle of love may come slowly. But there is no pattern of bondage to evil that necessitates some supplement to classic spiritual warfare. Occultists need repentance, not EMM.

Other New Testament passages discuss the occult, describing either repentance or judgment, but they never discuss EMM. Acts 19:11–20 is similar to Acts 8, if less detailed. In this passage the evil spirit is an immediate agent of affliction, acting on his own malice. When the people heard what happened they were struck with fear, magnified the name of Jesus, and repented of their occult practices. Instead of resorting to EMM, the answer to an occult lifestyle was classic spiritual warfare: the word of truth.

repentance, faith, worship, fear of God, and appropriate ioral change.

Earlier, in Acts 13:4–12, Paul rebuked Bar-Jesus, the ι. worker, in scorching terms. This son of the devil was judge immediately. There were no unclean spirits of bondage necessitating EMM, simply condemnation for this sorcerer's evil.

Revelation 9:20–21 speaks judgment on those who worship demons, serve idols, and do sorcery. The passage says twice that they did not repent. Although their practices put them into moral bondage to Satan, these practices did not enable enslaving spirits to infiltrate their hearts. EMM was not needed; they needed repentance.

Revelation 18 is extremely instructive on the relationship between unclean spirits and occult practices. God violently judged Babylon for using sorcery to deceive the nations and cursed Babylon with demons. Revelation 18 corroborates the view of indwelling evil spirits that we have seen repeatedly— they are not agents of sin, but agents of judgment and torment. Indwelling evil spirits are in the same category as vultures, plagues, torment, mourning, pestilence, famine, and burning— they are afflictions and curses (18:4–9). The demons and carrion eaters replace the joys of life: music, craftsmanship, productivity, food, light, and marital celebration (18:22–23). The Bible's view of unclean spirits is at odds with the view of demons that has become popular.

A final passage on the occult, Galatians 5:20, describes sorcery as a work of the flesh, coming from the lusts of the flesh. Sorcery is listed amid other sins, with no sense that the solution differs from how to deal with people who are sexually loose, get into arguments, or drink too much. Galatians 5:13–6:10 portrays classic-mode spiritual warfare, not EMM.

Similarly, the numerous passages that mention people coming out of idolatry bear on people emerging from involvement in the occult, because idolatry entails sacrifice to demons (1 Corinthians 10:20–21). When Paul warns against idolatry, he simply says, "Flee," naming numerous reasons and motives in the context (1 Corinthians 10:14). Earlier, Paul placed idolatry on the list of such sins as immorality, stealing, and drunkenness, speaking of the justifying and sanctifying power of the Spirit of God (1 Corinthians 6:9–11). The Corinthian situation was not unusual—most Gentile converts came from backgrounds in the degraded practices of idolatry.[7]

Intuitively, occult practices provide the strongest case for EMM theory. But Scripture views matters a different way. Given the occult, it tells us to speak the truth in love; worship and pray; reprove and warn; "show mercy, mixed with fear—hating even the clothing stained by corrupted flesh" (Jude 23).

What about Satan's Inworking Power of Moral Evil?

We have seen that demonization and ekballistics are consistently linked with situational evil. This, however, should not minimize our awareness of Satan's intimate involvement with the moral evil of the human soul. Advocates of the classic mode of spiritual warfare throughout history have been aware of the devil's hand in sin and unbelief. John Bunyan, for example, placed Diabolus's throne in the center of the town of Mansoul. Similarly, Thomas Brooks portrayed Satan insinuating sweet deceptions to the soul. And John Calvin wrote of the wretched state of humankind, "The devil has his throne within us, inhabits us body and soul! This makes God's mercy the more wonderful, that He converts us from Satan's stinking stables to His own temple and consecrates us as a spiritual habitation for himself."[8] Satan utterly rules his spiritual children, the seed of the serpent, children of their father the devil. But even we who have been born anew to become the children of God can still hear the voice of our former overlord.

Temptation is not purely external to us—the buddies at Joe's Bar, the pornographic magazine in the drugstore, the bombardment of Madison Avenue inducements to "need" whatever is sold, the subtleties of society and culture. Nor is temptation purely internal to our own soul—the lusts of the flesh that lead us astray and give birth to sins. Satan has means of addressing the soul with lies, of working on the inside.

This inworking power of moral evil does not call for EMM, as the following statements from Scripture make clear. Notice two things in each example. First, Satan's power to influence and enslave the inner life is vividly portrayed—he snatches away truth, inserts lies, blinds minds, holds people in bondage. Second, the classic mode of ministry in all its vigor, without a hint of EMM, is the solution.

- The devil takes the word of God from the hearts of people so that they will not believe and be saved. Yet the solution is to receive the word, hold it fast, and bear fruit patiently.[9]

- When Satan put it in the heart of Judas to betray Jesus and when he filled Ananias's heart to lie the result was death, not demons.[10]

- Although Satan actually entered Judas, working in him to murder Jesus, what resulted was severe condemnation for one who was earlier called a devil and later called a "son of perdition."[11]

- All human beings are blind, living under the dominion of Satan, but the answer is to turn to the light and receive forgiveness and an inheritance by faith.[12]

- The god of this world blinds the minds of the unbelieving that they might not see the light of the gospel of the glory of Christ; they will perish in their culpable unbelief.[13]

- All human beings live life according to the prince of the power of the air; they need to receive the life-giving power, love, and grace of God through faith.[14]

- Some people are held captive in the snare of the devil to do his will; they need to be corrected with gentleness that they might come to their senses, being granted repentance leading to knowledge of the truth.[15]

In each of these passages, the power of Satan to inwork moral evil could not be stated more vigorously. This is moral bondage. The intimacy of Satan's hand in evil is so immediate that it is no surprise that some people might appear to have demons of sin. People exhibit their bondage to sin and sin's uncanny master. Sin's ultimate logic is a "demonic wisdom," a culpable insanity of evil.

Yet the Bible repeatedly holds out a message of personal responsibility and classic-mode spiritual warfare. It is always *our* moral evil, *our* unbelief, pride, lusts, fears, and wickedness that need to be repented of. Moral bondage to the devil is simultaneously a slavery to the enthralling power of sin. The Bible often talks about our responsibility without mentioning the devil,[16] but the Bible never talks about the devil without mentioning our responsibility. The Bible does not portray moral evil—however heinous or devilish—as a demonization to be cast out. We minister to blind slaves with all the energies of prayer, love, and truth, fighting spiritual warfare in the classic mode.

EMM advocates frequently employ a form of logic that creates mischief and confusion. They say that if Satan is active, then EMM is both warranted and necessary. As a corollary, to oppose EMM is to view Satan and his demons as essentially inactive. This is called an "is-ought" argument: because something *is* so, therefore we necessarily *ought* to do such and such about it. As a corollary, to deny that we ought to do such and such is to deny that the problem exists.

Clearly, Satan *is* active as a liar and moral overlord, plunging people into iniquity. And clearly Satan *is* a murderer and torturer who seeks to hurt people. But it does not follow clearly that therefore we *ought* to do EMM. In fact Scripture teaches something very different. *Is* does not determine *ought*; the *ought*

needs to be examined directly. In teaching us to reclaim spiritual warfare, the Bible indicates that Satan *is* closely entangled
with the moral evil of the human soul, therefore we *ought* to do
classic-mode spiritual warfare.

We have covered a lot of ground. We next move on to a
discussion of how the epistles describe our spiritual warfare and
teach us to fight.

8

"RESIST THE DEVIL"

EKBALLISTIC WORKS APPEAR in Matthew, Mark, Luke, and Acts; demon deliverance does not appear in the rest of the New Testament.[1] Just as ekballistic encounters appeared dramatically when we turned from Malachi to Matthew, they dramatically disappear when we turn from Acts to Romans. In this chapter we will consider only the highlights of the scores of passages from Romans through Revelation that deal with Satan—his attacks, threats, the kind of bondage he seeks to establish, and how we should fight him. Understanding how to *resist* the devil is the key to reclaiming spiritual warfare in our day.

THE EPISTLES AND SITUATIONAL EVIL

The epistles[2] heavily focus on the warfare with moral evil—Satan's power to deceive us. But first we will briefly look at how they treat Satan's power to hurt and kill. In several places the epistles connect Satan and his demons to situational evil as sources of suffering, torment, and death. In Hebrews 2:14 the devil is described as the one who held the power of death but has been rendered powerless by the cross and resurrection of Christ for those who live by faith. Satan's ability to terrorize people with the ultimate situational evil—death—has been broken.

Several passages describe Satan as a torturer who wreaks sufferings on people. In two passages dealing with church discipline

107

Paul refers to people who are "delivered over to Satan."[3] Far from being delivered *from* their demons, rebels are delivered *to* the devil. Being cast out of the body of Christ subjects a person to the terrors of death and accusation, to exclusion from the fellowship of light, and to other sufferings and the general disintegration of life. Both of these passages indicate a remedial, teaching purpose for delivering someone to Satan. It occurs for disciplinary, not punitive, purposes: "that his spirit may be saved" and "that they may be taught not to blaspheme."

The Bible also occasionally describes punitive purposes in a number of final-judgment passages: demons are inflicted on those who disobey God. Recall, for example, the discussion of Revelation 18 in the previous chapter. This figures prominently in the often-misinterpreted "seven worse spirits" (Matthew 12:43–45), which will be discussed in chapter 9. Another example is Matthew 18:34, in which the "torturers" facing the hypocritical, unforgiving servant possibly are demonic tormentors. The popular notion of demonic torments in hell has biblical warrant.

In one passage Paul speaks of Satan stopping him from visiting the believers in Thessalonica (1 Thessalonians 2:18). From the context, Paul appears to mean that Satan animated human enemies of the gospel who created difficulties for him, hindering his plans for advancing the gospel.

Many argue that Paul's "thorn in [the] flesh, a messenger of Satan to torment" him, provides a case for ongoing demon-induced suffering (2 Corinthians 12:7). This thorn was possibly a physical affliction—perhaps the problem Paul alluded to in Galatians 4:13–15. If this interpretation is right, it reinforces the conclusions we have already drawn. Satan's messengers are particularly associated with physical sufferings. Notice how the affliction bears no relation to moral evil, but is actually used by God to *protect* Paul from moral evil. In speaking of Satan's messenger, the passage sounds the notes of suffering, weakness, mistreatment, distress, and difficulty—not sin.

Arguments have also been made that the thorn refers to human opponents of the gospel who continually attacked Paul and sought to undo his ministry.[4] Persecutions and false teachers forced Paul to kill his pride by reinforcing a continual need for dependency on God. Several factors, however, lean against this view and favor the physical-ailment view. Second Corinthians 12:1–9 seems to focus on personal, private experience: the third heavens, the inward temptation to pride, the buffeting in Paul's own person and flesh, prayer three times for deliverance, and God's personal communication of reassurance. As Paul typically accepted persecutions as an apostle's public lot, it does seem surprising that he would pray three times for it to be taken away.

In either case, however Satan attacked, Paul responded to the suffering non-ekballistically. The malicious afflictions kept Paul humble and dependent. He prayed for God's power to set him free; God said "no," instructing Paul about his larger purposes. The epistles consistently approach situational evil without recourse to EMM.

THE EPISTLES AND MORAL EVIL

The epistles concentrate their attention on what we properly call spiritual *warfare*: our vulnerability to be taken captive to Satan to believe his lies and do his will. They present moral evil as a three-stranded braid of the world, the flesh, and the devil. Our social situation feeds us a stream of beguilements and threats; our own hearts gravitate to lies and lusts; the devil schemes to aggravate sin and unbelief. Moral evil is also monolithic—the world, the flesh, and the devil work in concert. The Bible differentiates the three strands of monolithic evil without dividing them. The Bible never teaches that we have three sorts of problems: one set termed world problems, a second set identified as flesh problems, and a third set called "spiritual" problems.

Frequently EMM practice siphons off "spiritual" problems into a special category. For normal problems, the devil is virtually nonoperative; for supernormal problems, the world and the flesh are virtually nonoperative. "Spiritual" problems are said to need ekballistic means. Because of the inherent fascination with the supernormal, demonic causes of bondage to sin are continually pursued.

Here is another instance where EMM advocates jump from *is* to *ought*. They stress that if we recognize and allow the inworking power of Satan, we will see a self-evident justification for EMM. But in doing so they neglect what the epistles actually teach about how to fight spiritual warfare against the one who schemes to exert dark lordship. They import from the gospels and Acts ekballistic means for redressing situational evil, failing to see that Satan's intimate voice and hand in moral evil are *always* linked to the flesh, and frequently linked to the world. And they fail to see that resisting Satan's intimate voice and hand in moral evil is *never* linked with ekballistic means.

Not only do the world, the flesh, and the devil appear in concert, but the Bible consistently presents them in a carefully crafted balance. Of the three, God primarily focuses on the flesh—the human heart and its vulnerability to evil. Humans stand center stage. We are called to radical self-knowledge in relation to the gospel of Christ's grace. We are called to search out all the corruption, deceit, and depravity of our hearts, hands, and tongues. We are called to know God in fellowship with our blood-bought brothers and sisters. Scripture addresses people, not demons.

With responsible humans at center stage, the world parades a supporting cast of villains, along with props and scenery. The world provides the situations that reveal and test the character of the protagonists. Scripture particularly focuses on false teachers, who mislead others by word and example, and on enemies, who oppress and hurt others. The world contains material objects as well as people: physical idols, money and goods, pictures and images, technological creations of countless sorts.

When we glimpse backstage we see the devil, who appears more frequently than in the Old Testament but still stands distinctly behind the scenes. Virtually every epistle mentions him once or twice; a few mention him more often; none, however, dwell on him. He is the tempter, accuser, and deceiver whose goal is moral lordship. He is the serial killer of all whom he entices into service; he would kill the saints if he could. To fight this adversary is simultaneously to fight both the world and the flesh. Satan's malice animates the world and beguiles the heart without ever making humans less than responsible for their iniquity. To fight conformity to and friendship with the world *is* to fight Satan. To fight the dark lies and lusts of the flesh *is* to fight Satan.

The balance within monolithic evil can be illustrated by several fictional portrayals of spiritual warfare. C. S. Lewis's space trilogy and J. R. R. Tolkien's *Lord of the Rings* show the proper balance. Frank Peretti's *This Present Darkness*, in contrast, skews the balance. For Lewis and Tolkien, human (or hobbit) beings stand front and center, creating a courageous fellowship of light amid a dark and dangerous world. Human choices and beliefs are all-important. The drama in the human soul is complex, rich, and at times ambivalent, unfolding through time and circumstance. Liars and attackers—varied social pressures and enemies—make up the supporting cast. Periodically we glimpse the malign spiritual force who holds the world in darkness: the dead man's head in *That Hideous Strength* and Sauron in *Lord of the Rings*. But Peretti inverts this emphasis. His demons are front and center as the most interesting and vivid characters in the drama. The world—the psychology department—operates in the middle ground. The human actors are all-or-nothing pawns of either the devil or the Holy Spirit. Peretti's one-dimensional human protagonists are as predictable as the Bible's demons.

The epistles set forth modes of ministry and life that address the complementary aspects of evil: the pressures of the world, the lusts of the flesh, the activities of the enemy. We will examine three passages that lift the curtain on the devil: Ephesians 6:10–20, 1 Peter 5:5–11, and James 3:13–4:12. One command stands out in each passage: "Resist." We will explore what we resist, what resistance and the failure to resist look like, ιe results of resistance.

IN THE FACE OF LIES, PAUL COMMANDS "RESIST!"

Ephesians chiefly stresses the attacks of deception that darken and harden people. Satan establishes his moral lordship mainly through lies.[5] His lies appeal to old cravings: for god-like autonomy, pleasure, power, self-righteousness, knowledge, glory, love, meaning. His lies also awaken fresh cravings. The intensity of our moral slavery to the master in the realm of the old self can hardly be overstated. Every intent of the thoughts of the heart is only evil continually.[6] But in the most famous and extended passage on spiritual warfare, Ephesians 6:10–20, Paul shows those whom God has made alive how to fight. In a word, he says "Resist." He then calls us to put on God's power and armor.

Notice first that Ephesians 6:10–20 does not introduce the subject of spiritual warfare in Paul's letter. Rather it sums up and crystallizes into a vivid image what Paul teaches throughout the entire letter. Satan's activities and strategies appear throughout Ephesians. And the inworking and protecting power of God, mentioned in 6:10, repeats a theme that also weaves through the entire book. Each piece of God's armor has already appeared in various forms in Paul's teaching and example.

We are to resist the powers of darkness that scheme against God's people.[7] These forces of wickedness are the same spiritual powers that Christ has subjected by his power (1:21) and will witness the triumph of God's wisdom in the church (3:10). These powers are ruled by the prince of the power of the air (2:2) who works in those who are disobedient. This devil seeks to use our sins to destroy the work of God, to fragment the unity of the body of Christ (4:27).

Ephesians gives no hint that the prince of evil's schemes and flaming missiles involve demonization. In comparison to other New Testament epistles, the letter rarely mentions suffering, instead focusing almost exclusively on our moral conflict and vulnerability to deception. The issue in view is human moral evil.

The devil's schemes seek to draw us into sin and lies, to harden and darken us, to induce us to live in the flesh. Chapter 2 confirms this in its description of the results of the devil's activity: trespasses, sins, disobedient children, followers of lusts, people under the wrath of God for sin. It is also confirmed by chapter 4, where the word "schemes" describes the deceitfulness of the world in drawing us away from Christ's truth (4:14; see also 5:6). And it is confirmed by the entire discussion in 4:17–6:9 where Paul speaks the truth in love to build up the body of Christ. These chapters are an extended meditation on themes introduced in 2:1–10. We witness the devil's inworking power as we observe the flesh; we witness God's inworking power as we observe faith and good works.

Throughout Ephesians Paul himself exemplifies spiritual warfare in action: with loins girded with truth he teaches the way of righteousness, brings the gospel of peace to the nations, lives by faith in the power of God, rejoices in salvation, wields the sword of the Spirit, and prays fervently for God's people to grow in the knowledge of Christ and in his power. Paul destroys deceptive words and dark works; he teaches God's children to walk in the light of Jesus. The entire letter illustrates, by precept and example, how to resist the devil

When one of the devil's schemes succeeds and a flaming missile hits we do not *acquire* evil alien inhabitants. Rather we become *like* the evil alien. Various sordid aspects of failing to resist are outlined in almost every verse from 4:17–6:9 in the descriptions of the way the nations and the flesh live. Resistance, in contrast, appears throughout Ephesians 1–6 in the positive descriptions of the Christian life.

The armor described in 6:10–20 is the armor that God himself wears, just as the power is God's own power. As we have noted before, New Testament spiritual warfare deepens Old Testament warfare. When Jesus resisted the devil in the desert, he fought spiritual warfare as found in Deuteronomy. In Ephesians spiritual warfare occurs in the Isaiah mode.

Each of the pieces of armor is rooted in the Old Testament, mainly Isaiah. Note that the *Messiah* girds his loins with the truth by fearing God and walking in the power and wisdom of the Spirit (11:5).[8] The LORD God puts on the breastplate of righteousness to deliver his people from bondage to sins (59:17).[9] The LORD himself comes—his feet shod—bearing good news of peace to those captivated in sin and judgment (52:7).[10] In the one piece of weaponry not rooted in Isaiah the LORD himself is the shield behind which faith takes refuge from enemies.[11] The LORD wears the helmet of salvation as he brings deliverance from the power of sin and gives his Spirit and Word (59:17).[12] The sword of the Spirit is God's Word and proceeds from the mouth of the *Messiah*, the Servant who will deliver the nations from the power of darkness (49:2).[13]

Prayer is the way all this happens, for prayer relies on the Lord. To take up the armor is to "put on the Lord Jesus Christ" in order not to be captivated to the flesh, as Paul puts it in Romans 13:14. To take up the armor is simply to live *in Christ*.

Through the classic mode of spiritual warfare portrayed in this passage we learn how to "stand" and wage successful warfare. The enemy lies at our feet defeated. When we live by faith and love we *stand* on the battlefield. This does not mean, however, that a Christian is invulnerable or insulated to dark persuasions. If that were true, Scripture would not need to warn us of the nature of our battle with the world, the flesh, and the devil.

The ekballistic literature, in contrast, teaches that enemy agents worm in until they are discovered and routed out. EMM warfare claims to deliver us from the grip of foes *concealed* within human nature. But classic warfare—the picture Paul paints—delivers us from the grip of foes *revealed* by human nature. Those who are new creations learn to live in the light, standing against the darkness.

IN THE MIDST OF SUFFERING,
PETER COMMANDS "RESIST!"

Ephesians addresses the saints in a world of beguilement; 1 Peter addresses saints in a world of oppression.[14] Both epistles assume that the warfare is for the human heart: lies and lusts compete with truth and love. 1 Peter 5:8 contains the letter's only mention of the evil one, a vivid reference: "Your enemy the devil prowls around like a roaring lion looking for someone to devour." Peter gives pithy advice: "Resist him, standing firm in the faith, because you know that your brothers throughout the world are undergoing the same kind of sufferings."

Like Paul in Ephesians 6, Peter is not introducing a new theme at the end of his letter. Rather he deepens our understanding of the central theme of the book. In the first four chapters he writes of the suffering that purifies faith, of how to glorify God amid suffering, of trusting God and pursuing good while suffering, of the inevitability of suffering. Then in chapter 5 he reveals the spirit adversary who stands behind the fiery ordeal of persecution.

Lying and persecution are complementary strategies that aim at the same result: unbelief and sin. Lies are the "carrot" of temptation; sufferings are the "stick." Lies lure us with false promises while sufferings threaten us. Betrayals, beatings, threats, brutalities, violence, enmity, and abuse produce a host of temptations, such as revenge, fear, bitterness, and despair. Peter is writing to believers tempted by suffering. In the immediate context, the roaring lion seeks to kill believers. By so doing he aims to compromise their faith, make them revile their revilers, and force them to fear their enemies.

Some EMM advocates say that to be "devoured" by the lion means to become demonized. But this misses both the immediate and larger context. The ravenous lion is a common biblical metaphor for those who hurt and oppress God's people. Jesus himself faced the lion when he was mocked and crucified.[15] In many of the Messianic psalms, a lion prowls after the afflicted

one who hopes in the LORD.[16] Both in the Psalms and in 1 Peter
these enemies are most evidently human—the world. But in 1
Peter 5:8 we glimpse the choreographer of malice.

If warfare in Matthew 4 arises from Deuteronomy and Ephesians 6 from Isaiah, then 1 Peter 5 wages war in the Psalms
mode. In each of the passages about the prowling lion, the
psalmist fights by finding refuge in God himself. He sets his heart
to hope steadfastly in God's promises amid pain and danger; he
worships. First Peter 5 is filled with instructions on how to fight.
Faith trusts God's proper time of deliverance (5:6). Faith finds
freedom from care, taking refuge in God's tender concern (5:7).
Faith maintains an alert hold on reality when the lion slashes
(5:8). Faith stands, unsurprised by persecutions, setting its hope
firmly on the grace to be revealed in Christ (5:9–10). Faith worships him to whom belongs dominion forever and ever—Amen
(5:11). Each of these themes in 1 Peter expresses the faith of
the Psalms. The very sufferings by which Satan would brutalize us
into his image are used by God to purify our faith and reveal his
glory. As in Job and all of Scripture, the malice of the devil ultimately serves the very cause he hates.

Failing to resist in the face of threat appears throughout the
whole letter in the discussions of lusts, malice, guile, reviling,
fear, dissipation, anxiety, and pride. To be devoured is simply to
return evil for evil; to become a being who thinks and acts like
the devil.

Through successful resistance, in contrast, God himself will
perfect, confirm, strengthen, and establish us. The devil is
defeated and God glorified. Like Ephesians 6, 1 Peter 5 teaches
classic-mode spiritual warfare: the clear-headed dependency and
practical obedience of faith. Those who take refuge in the LORD
find a haven from the lion's malice and bid for lordship.

Many EMM books mock this dependency, as though asking
God for help communicates a stance of childish weakness, fear,
and defeat. They say that God calls us to grow up and "take
authority" over the powers of darkness. From this stance of
authority we should then bind and cast out the demons of moral

slavery that threaten and inhabit us. This may sound persuasive until we realize that our Lord and his apostles teach us something different. Faith undoubtedly has an unshakable confidence in God's promises and power and is triumphant over evil; mature faith exhibits a certain fearless authority.

But Jesus, Paul, and Peter, like the Psalms, teach and practice a mode of spiritual warfare that is fundamentally "weak"—that is, reliant on God. When the messenger of Satan pierced Paul with a thorn, Paul interceded three times, then learned to say, "When I am weak, then I am strong." When the roaring lion tore into Jesus' body, Jesus said, "Father, into your hands I commit my spirit." He was raised triumphant through the power of the Holy Spirit.

IN THE PRESENCE OF THE FLESH, JAMES COMMANDS "RESIST!"

"Resist" is what Paul said regarding the carrot the liar dangles in front of the donkey. "Resist" is what Peter said regarding the stick with which the murderer beats the donkey. And "resist" is also what James says. He, however, focuses on the donkey itself: the human heart.[17] James does not specifically link the devil with trials and sufferings, but instead links the devil directly with our sinfulness.[18] The devil only has a foothold for persuasion or intimidation because of our hearts' congruence with his intentions. In James 4:7 we hear the familiar song of spiritual warfare: "Resist the devil, and he will flee from you."

We are to resist Satan as he works with our moral folly and appeals to our cravings. James 1:14–15 clearly sets forth the basic problem. We are tempted when our own cravings carry us away; cravings beget sin, and sin issues in death. Throughout the entire letter, James details our primary sins and self-deceptions. Toward the end of chapter 3 he shows that "wisdom" from our proud and foolish hearts is actually rooted in the devil (3:15). Finally in 4:7, James, like Paul and Peter, says to resist the devil. Spiritual realities and warfare are not just appearing now, halfway through the letter. As with Paul and Peter, the discussion of James's entire book is enriched by a glimpse backstage.

The failure to resist can be seen in the following manifestations of demonic folly: an incendiary tongue (3:1–12), a demanding and self-exalting heart that produces chaos and every evil practice (3:14–16), cravings that produce interpersonal conflict (4:1–3), spiritual adultery and hostility against God (4:4), pride (4:6), double-minds and dirty hands (4:8), playing God (4:11–12), and arrogantly forgetting that God holds our existence in his hands (4:13–17). Amid these descriptions of evil, it would be incongruous for the references to the devil suddenly to introduce the danger of inhabiting unclean spirits. James is dealing with a much bigger issue: the moral conformity of our inner and outer lives to the image of Satan.

In resisting the devil James teaches classic-mode spiritual warfare, not EMM. He appeals first to God the giver, who freely bestows grace and wisdom to those who ask.[19] God's gift produces wise people who are obedient, gentle, reasonable, merciful, unwavering, and able to make peace in a world of war (3:17–18). James shows the generous power of God: "He gives a greater grace" (4:6, NASB). In the midst of all the sordid, demonic, and degraded folly, this short sentence is one of the sweetest in Scripture. God's grace is greater—greater than this present darkness. Then James teaches us how to repent and draw near to God (4:7–10). Resisting the devil is part of it; he says to resist falling into the image of demonic folly and resist the temptations that arise in our own heart. James teaches the classic mode of warfare in its distilled essence: repentance, faith, and action.

When we resist the devil's attempt to seize moral control, James promises that "he will flee from you." The promise of victory could not be stronger. Classic-mode warfare is the power encounter that shatters the devil's kingdom of lies and death. Victory in war comes when repentant and believing refugees from the dominion of darkness embrace the power of God. This is the way the prayerful have always fought their enemies and triumphed: Job, David, Jeremiah, Habakkuk, Daniel, Jesus, Paul, Peter, James. And it is the way that we today must fight to win.

James's mode of warfare is based on themes throughout the Old Testament and from the teachings of Jesus (particularly in Matthew). But perhaps Proverbs stands out. The way of victory in war is the way of wisdom in life. The worldview and practices of Proverbs 2, 3, and 4 breathe throughout James. Spiritual warfare is the blood, sweat, and tears of dying to one's self and listening to God. When Satan holds out the carrot of lies, resist. When Satan hammers us with the stick of suffering, resist. When the donkey would act like the devil, resist. Those who draw near to God in repentant faith encounter the power who enables them to live in obedient faith.

DEMONICALLY INDUCED AFFLICTION

Before we move on from the epistles, we should explore how to address demonically induced afflictions. Notice first that the *vast* majority of cases of "demonization" cited by EMM practitioners are cases of misdiagnosis. What is called a demon usually is a manifestation of sinful fear, bitterness, craving, unbelief, and the like.

But what about the remaining cases where people may suffer demon-produced afflictions? What about nonmoral, physical effects of Satan's malice, such as deafness, dumbness, paralysis, convulsions? Or such mental effects as dementia and bizarre behavior not connected to moral or physiological causes? How should we address these problems, where physical diseases and demonic torment produce similar miseries? Here is another place where both proponents and opponents of EMM have to interpret the relative silence of Scripture. How should we help the demonically afflicted? Second Corinthians 12 gave us many hints, as we saw earlier in this chapter. But the clearest answer lies in the letter we have just been looking at—James.

Using the close analogy between sickness, the weather, and demonic suffering, the proper treatment in such cases is roughly what James 5:14–18 sets forth. Three components stand out: first, fervent, believing prayer with the sufferer for God's healing mercy; second, an exploration of possible medical causes and treatments, applied as appropriate in the Lord's name; and third, probing pastoral care to turn these adverse circumstances into an opportunity for ongoing repentance and growth in grace.

The guidelines found in James 5 have many implications and applications. For example, some cultures and individuals live in a world of superstitious fears, tending to overinterpret sickness and other hardships as demonic. Other cultures and individuals are skeptical about unclean spirits, and tend not to notice demonic activity. The pattern of ministry set forth in James 5 applies equally well in either case. The combination of fervent prayer, the best available medicine, and wise counsel would do what can be done for both strictly physical ailments and spirit agents of affliction. From the standpoint of what human helpers should do, there is no *significant* difference between demonization and sickness, either in symptoms or cure.

By analogy, some Christians interpret hindrances to ministry as demonically inspired while others interpret hindrances naturalistically. In either case, knowing this is *God's* world lets us arrive at a common mode. Determining whether or not there is a "demon in the toaster"—or simply a loose wire—is less important than how one deals with it. Both EMM and prayerless reliance on technical expertise are defective responses. When the missionaries' movie projector does not work and they learn that the local witch doctor has cursed their meeting, they should both cry out to God for help and check their wiring.

RETHINKING
THE DETAILS

THUS FAR WE HAVE VIEWED EMM in broad strokes. Now we will look more closely at the details of contemporary ekballistic thinking and practice. Not all comments, of course, will apply to every practitioner. But the following eight questions probe aspects of EMM practice that are widespread and deserve attention.

1. "WHAT ABOUT THE TOUGH CASES?"

Christians who get involved in EMM inevitably have a story to tell. These stories have a number of common features. EMM practitioners are pastorally oriented—they want to help people and spread the knowledge of Christ. Typically they have encountered tough cases where the pat answers did not work. The frustrating cases led them to question their operative practical theology. They became open to new ways that promised greater effectiveness.

The place of stories in EMM is so decisive that it becomes difficult to argue against them. After all, on what basis can we question another's story without seeming arrogant and unbelieving? Can I presume that *my* story, which reached an opposite conclusion, is somehow superior? If matters stay at the level of competing stories, we have only two options: either all is relative or one of us is benighted.[1] We all need absolute biblical truth to engage us in our stories and in a process of correction. The following four observations should help readers evaluate the stories with a proper balance of charity and critique.

First, truth and error often coexist in sincere Christians.[2] EMM advocates typically believe in classic-mode spiritual warfare, which serves them well in much of life. But in certain situations they overlay the classic mode onto a theory of demonized sin. Or they add the ekballistic mode to the classic mode, without differentiating what the Bible teaches about the purposes and focus of each. This creates a practical theology that mixes incompatible ideas and practices. One can disagree with distinctives without dismissing those commonalities that stand in happy contradiction to the distinctions.

Second, erroneous views may operate as metaphors for valuable truths that are not put in a more orthodox fashion. I do not mean that error is not serious, or that everything is simply a matter of perspective, with all perspectives equally valid. But some errors have better intentions than other errors. For example, the idea of demonized sin may serve EMM practitioners as a way to crystallize both the complexity of sin and Satan's inworking hand in moral evil. Because their operative view of sin itself tends to be somewhat superficial they need a category to cover the deep bondage to darkness.

Most EMM advocates have a "Pelagian" view of sin: they believe that sin consists of conscious willed actions where one could have chosen the alternative. That definition works well for some sins—the high-handed sins mentioned in Psalm 19:13. But it is inadequate for the "bondage of the will," the deep compulsions, the habitual and instinctive darkness of the human soul—as described in Genesis 6:5, Psalm 19:12, Ecclesiastes 9:3, Ephesians 4:17–22, and James 3:14–4:12. The Augustinian view of sin, by contrast, takes seriously both willed sin and blind willfulness. The EMM view of demonized sin is an inadequate way of accounting for "dark things" on the human soul; it substitutes for Augustinian self-knowing. Although the Pelagian view is inadequate and misleading, it is not necessarily fatal to vital Christian life.

Third, an examination of what EMM advocates react *against* typically shows an impoverished employment of classic-mode spiritual warfare. On inspection, the classic mode—words of truth, faith, repentance, prayer, and obedience—is truncated to such things as verbally renouncing sin, desiring to "let go and let God," exerting will power, memorizing Bible verses, studying to gain rational doctrinal knowledge, becoming involved in formal ministry, and maintaining basic Christian disciplines. Not surprisingly, when such diminished forms of piety, volition, rationality, activism, and technique do not solve the tough problems, people turn to EMM. The inadequacy lies not in the classic mode, but in the church's poor appropriation of that mode in all its subtlety and power.

Typical descriptions of the practices purported to have failed often reveal a lack of genuine self-knowledge and pastoral insight. One example is the truncated definition of repentance that many EMM practitioners hold. Many begin a counseling process by working through a detailed list of occult and cultic activities along with other sins. The counselee checks off the ones that apply and prays prescribed prayers of repentance. He or she renounces these sinful things, claiming certain promises and protections. Such renunciations—whether mechanical or earnest—may occasionally create a significant breaking point with a particular sin, but generally do not work for the ongoing battle with sin. The classic mode seems to have failed, when actually it has been used superficially. Then other explanations and techniques start to sound attractive.

Fourth, as I read and listened to EMM advocates tell their stories, I remember thinking to myself, "Where have I heard this before?" Then I realized that Christians who turn toward secular psychology tell the same stories. Those who find "deeper" explanations in psychology and "more powerful" methods in psychotherapy mirror the stories of EMM advocates. Their understanding of sin and their way of using the classic mode similarly reveal superficiality. They too want greater explanatory insight and greater power to effect change in themselves and others. They too have encountered tough cases, bizarre emotions, and behavioral and mental slaveries. They too see "dark things" in the soul that their definitions of sin and misery cannot account for or solve.

One set of believers has turned to psychodynamic explanations for "emotional" problems and to therapy; the other set has turned to demonic explanations for "spiritual" problems and to power encounters. Psychotherapy and EMM both miss the third way that provides the true power encounter with moral evil: reclaiming the classic mode of spiritual warfare. There is also a current trend to combine the therapeutic with the ekballistic, joining two misguided approaches. These tendencies surface, for example, in James Friesen, Fred Dickason, and Ed Murphy.

2. "SHOULD WE NAME DEMONS?"

What categories should we use to diagnose people's deep-seated problems? The "normal" categories consist of behavioral sins and do not probe the briar patches and mud wallows of the human soul. When people get scratched by the thorns and are stuck in the mud they search for help. The therapeutic approach offers one beguiling set of explanations in which psychological jargon proliferates syndromes and diagnoses that pretend to give explanatory insight. The EMM approach goes in the opposite direction and gives names to supposed demonic agencies.

The proof text for identifying deep-seated problems with the names of demons is Mark 5:9. Jesus asked the Gadarene demoniac, "What is your name?" The demon replied, "Legion, for we are many."[3] EMM practitioners believe that this verse teaches us to identify demons by name. Accordingly EMM practitioners find demons named Anger, Hate, Self-Pity, Pride, Fear, Fear of Others, Rebellion, Unbelief, Lust, Suicide, Homosexuality, Despair, Resentment, Tongues, Non-acceptance, Liar, Self-hate, and so forth. They also find demons matching the varied names the Bible attaches to the evil one: Lucifer, Beelzebub, Satan, Apollyon.

EMM ministers employ widely differing techniques to identify the particular demon inhabitants. At one end of the spectrum are the gentle therapeutic workers. Fred Dickason has counselees relax and asks them to free associate. Persistent or obsessive topics then reveal the locations and identities of demons. Neil Anderson asks people to notice when they experience an inner opposition to what he is saying. Demonic agents reside in the places charged with emotionally charged false beliefs. At the other end of the spectrum are the ekballistic power workers who use revelations or who, like Don Basham, command any demons present to manifest themselves.

But what is the significance of Jesus' question: "What is your name?" Was he teaching us to identify names of demons as a pastoral method? Was he asking in order to enter into conversation with the demons? Did he connect demons to patterns of sin in the demonized? Notice that Jesus never received a name for an answer; he got a number. Perhaps Jesus never intended to hear an actual name. Scripture never names any demons except their chief. The demons always obeyed Jesus, so if a name was needed it would have been forthcoming.

Jesus did not seek a supposed moral ground or right by which the demon had taken up residency in the man. Was the demoniac a particularly great sinner? Had he been traumatically sinned against? Were his ancestors occult power workers? Scripture neither gives us clues nor shows any interest in these questions. A great deal of ekballistic energy has been spent doing things that Mark 5:9 never envisions. EMM distinctives are brought *to* the verse rather than being learned *from* the verse.

EMM ministries differ widely regarding how much they talk to demons. Neil Anderson, for example, has moved completely away from naming and conversing with demons. Fred Dickason, on the other hand, converses extensively with demons and even seeks demonic corroboration for particular doctrines he holds. Overall, most EMM ministries are now downplaying conversations with demons.

EMM ministries typically deal with people's besetting sins. Case studies and summaries redefine these routine sins of the heart as ruler demons: hate, self-pity, pride, fear, fear of people, rebellion, unbelief, and lust. They overlay their view of demonized sin onto accessible and typical human experience.

The techniques of identifying "demons" by free association, noting inner opposition, and coming up with diagnostic words of knowledge are easy to replicate even if we do not believe in demonized sin. For example, relax, unhinge conscious control, and free associate for five minutes. Your besetting sins and unresolved relationships will soon come up. But are these demons? Or notice when your mind rears up with an emotionally charged "but" at God's call to let go of bitterness toward another. The lies of the devil to which you listen will soon appear. But are these demons? Or take a stab at determining another person's besetting sins. This is not particularly difficult, especially when troubled people seek help. Is such discernment a word of knowledge about demon inhabitants or simply insight into another's struggles?

3. "CAN WE INHERIT DEMONS FROM OUR ANCESTORS?"

A frequently cited cause of demonized Christians is demons inherited from ancestors. If someone's ancestor used Ouija boards, practiced witchcraft, or lived an immoral life, the person may have acquired demons that harass and hold him or her in bondage to sins. A leading EMM teacher put it this way: "I have found this avenue of ancestral involvement to be *the chief cause of demonization*. Well over 95 percent of more than 400 persons I have contacted in my counseling ministry have been demonized because of their ancestors' involvement in occult and demonic activities."[4]

The proof text for transgenerational demons is Exodus 20:5, part of the Ten Commandments. The command against idolatry closes with this warning: the LORD is a jealous God, "punishing the children for the sins of the fathers to the third and fourth generations of those who hate me." This threat of judgment is

interpreted as a warrant for demons passed down the famil
although this idea appears nowhere in the Bible. Exodu
simply means what it seems to say: sin will be judged. Th
Testament provides repeated instances of idolaters reaping
destruction with moral decay and violent death extending to
their descendants. But nowhere in the Old Testament is this
connected with demons of moral bondage being passed down
through the generations. The notion of generational transfer-
ence of demonic agents is quite simply a piece of occult theology
that has infiltrated the EMM worldview.

4. "Are There Stages of Demonization?"

Many EMM books teach a developmental sequence of demonization by assembling a series of proof texts. There are many
variants, but a typical view says that oppression (Acts 10:38)
leads to a foothold or ground (Ephesians 4:27) leads to a stronghold (2 Corinthians 10:4) leads to full demonization or even
possession (gospels). Moral slavery is the end result of a multi-
stage process.

The process is said to begin with oppressive temptations,
blasphemous thoughts, and lies from the devil. If someone enter-
tains or engages in these, the demons gain a foothold—a moral
ground. And if the person continues to yield to occult practice,
believe lies, nurse anger, and indulge in sexual sin, the foothold
becomes a stronghold. Christians are typically seen as somewhere on the oppression-foothold-stronghold spectrum. The key
to conducting ekballistic ministry is to identify what ground the
devil owns, determine how the foothold was established, and
then cast out the demon.

This part of EMM theory offers an extremely graphic
metaphor for sin's moral invasion and the sinner's moral decline
into servitude. But they take their metaphor as reality, proceed-
ing to cast out demons that are actually deeply entrenched sins.
This moral slavery, listening to the deceits Satan whispers, is
exactly what classic-mode spiritual warfare addresses.

EMM proponents cite Acts 10:38, Ephesians 4:27, and 2 Corinthians 10:4 as proof texts. But none of these passages teach anything related to stages of demonization. Acts 10:38 says that Jesus "went about doing good and healing all who were under the power of the devil, because God was with him." This refers to Jesus' ekballistic healings. The rest of Peter's speech to the Gentiles (10:34–43) shows how the gospel deals with moral evil. But this one verse confirms Jesus' divine power and goodness in redressing human suffering. The mode of ministry and warfare taught in Acts 10 is the classic mode: repent, believe, and do right.

Another much-quoted passage is Ephesians 4:27, which says, "Do not give the devil a foothold." The idea that sin gives the devil a psychological foothold or "ground" is omnipresent in EMM thinking. But does this passage actually say anything of the sort? Ephesians 4 focuses on the church as a body working well together, being built up in the unity of the Spirit. Various sins shatter this unity, with lies and anger chief among such sins (4:25–27, 29–31). When a Christian does not solve a problem that has led to anger, the body is threatened. The devil gets a foothold in the church for his agenda: division.[5] Speaking the truth in love builds up the church; speaking falsehood and anger tears the church down. Ephesians 4:27 offers no support for a theory that the devil acquires psychological space, makes an invasionary landing, and takes ownership over part of a person's life. And the passage clearly teaches the classic mode of ministry: put off the old lifestyle, inside and out, and put on the new by the power of Christ, for by so doing the body of Christ will be built up.

Second Corinthians 10:4 is similar: "The weapons we fight with are not the weapons of the world. On the contrary, they have divine power to demolish strongholds." The strongholds are false teachings that Paul casts down by speaking the truth openly, a theme that has appeared repeatedly in this letter. This passage has nothing directly to do with demons. Certainly the serpent *is* a deceiver (2 Corinthians 11:3) and false teachers *are* Satan's servants (2 Corinthians 11:13–15). But Paul is talking to the Corinthians to alert them to the schemes of their spirit and human enemies who would put them in bondage to lies. Second Corinthians 10:4 has nothing to do with a part of our psyche that a demon might reign over. To teach EMM from this passage fishes for a proof text to validate a theory constructed of extra-biblical materials. The mode of ministry taught in the context is the classic mode: speak truth faithfully, repent from error, learn simple and pure devotion to Christ.

The series of proof texts we have considered does not deliver an explanation for supposed moral demonization. The Bible is utterly silent on the question of how those demonizations in the gospels arose. The safest answer, given the totality of what Scripture *does* reveal, is Jesus' response to his disciples regarding the man born blind: "Neither this man nor his parents sinned, but this happened so that the work of God might be displayed in his life" (John 9:3).

The causes of demonization are one of the Bible's many curiosity-provoking silences regarding the devil and his hosts. We dare not satisfy curiosity through speculation nor construct a comprehensive pastoral theology from fancies. But the Bible speaks volumes about how our moral enslavement to the devil occurs, instructing us about the classic mode of spiritual warfare as the power of deliverance.

5. "Should We Bind Demons?"

EMM practice is distinctive not only when it names demons and describes how we acquire them but in the way it seeks to get rid of them decisively. Typically the deliverance minister "binds" the spirits through various commands and prayers. The chief proof text for this practice is Matthew 12:29: "Or again, how can anyone enter a strong man's house and carry off his possessions unless he first ties up the strong man? Then he can rob his house." This is often supplemented by Matthew 16:19 and 18:18 where Jesus says, "whatever you bind on earth will be bound in heaven." Ekballistics take place, its advocates claim, by binding the powers of evil, repudiating the ground they hold within the demonized, and commanding them to leave.

Matthew 12:29, however, has been wrenched completely out of context and made to justify a great deal of superstition. Verbal formulas of "binding" demons have the ring of magical formulas, not biblical ministry of the Word. The passage does not intend to describe pastoral methodology; rather, it is a parable describing Jesus' cosmic work as the Messiah. He entered a "house" that belonged to a "strongman" whom he "tied up" in order to "rob" him of his "possessions." The house is planet earth. The strongman is Satan. The possessions are people, you and I, whom Jesus has saved, robbing the devil. The tying up is the entire work of Christ—from ekballistic foretastes of mercy to his death on the cross to his resurrection. Satan's kingdom of sin and death has been dealt a definitive blow, and his former followers are fleeing the darkness and streaming into the kingdom of mercy, righteousness, and life. The passage does not teach—and nowhere else does Jesus illustrate—a pastoral method of "binding" spirits.

Matthew 16:19 and 18:18 speak of both binding and loosing, and these verbal formulas often find their way into EMM practice. But are these passages about EMM? Do they have anything at all to do with demons? In fact, the binding and loosing refer to *people* being either inside or outside the community of God, not to spirits being inside or outside individuals. These are the only two passages where Jesus uses the word "church." He refers to the work of the church as God's steward holding the "keys": defining right and wrong, defining people as inside or outside the community, defining who is or is not forgiven.

6. "DO WE NEED CONTINUED SELF-DELIVERANCES?"

Another prominent feature of ekballistic counseling is self-deliverance. People are taught to "maintain their deliverance" against the danger of reinvasion. The proof text most often given is Matthew 12:43–45. In this parable, Jesus tells what happens when an unclean spirit is cast out. Eventually it comes back to its original home, and finding it empty, it "takes with it seven other spirits more wicked than itself, and they go in and live there. And the final condition of that man is worse than the first." EMM practitioners use this passage to warn that people who do not maintain their deliverance are liable to fall into a worse state of bondage to demons of sin. Because of the danger of reinvasion, EMM teaches techniques of ongoing self-protection and self-deliverance. Many of these techniques involve elements of classic-mode discipleship—truth, Bible study, prayer, repentance, worship—along with EMM warfare techniques. All these are overlaid on the EMM worldview.[6]

But Matthew 12:43–45 is actually a parable. Jesus is not teaching about ekballistics, but about what will happen to people who do not listen to him: "That is how it will be with this wicked generation." In the previous ten verses Jesus has been calling people to repent because "something greater" is here. Matthew 12:43–45 provides the climax to this vigorous call to wake up and repent: Jesus warns that the unrepentant will perish. The seven wicked spirits picture hell, not some temporal state of reinvasion. Jesus is casting out afflicting spirits, but if people do not repent, they face final affliction. The seven spirits are God's judgment on the sin of unbelieving Israel, bringing worse misery. The passage is about the nation of Israel and the judgment day, not about the "psychology" of spiritual warfare.

interesting

This passage is consistent with what we saw about the demonizations in the gospels as sufferings of the curse. Jesus used those foretastes of hell to demonstrate his tangible power to bring blessings of life, health, and freedom. But they also pointed to the bigger threat: The problem of moral evil warrants the varied forms of God's curse on sinners, unless sinners repent. The EMM notion of maintaining one's deliverance is made a substitute for the self-examination, ongoing repentance, fervent prayer, and worship of the classic mode.

EMM practitioners propose an entire worldview and system of pastoral practice, but, point by point, their distinctive ideas and methods fail the test of Scripture. Scripture explicitly teaches us many things about spiritual warfare, but demons of sin, ancestral spirits, stages of demonization, binding unclean spirits, and maintaining one's deliverance do not derive from the proof texts that supposedly support these ideas.

7. "IF IT'S WRONG, WHY DID IT WORK FOR ME?"

What about when EMM changes people? Do anecdotes of successful outcomes vindicate EMM? This is a challenging question. It is hard to argue with success.

God may well use EMM to help people, because good elements intermingle with the problematic distinctives. God inevitably uses means that are more or less off target as he accomplishes his work—which of us does ministry exactly as Jesus or Paul would? This does not mean we should recommend the erroneous, but rather that we must make our assessments in charity. The intermingling of good and bad also means the EMM movement has a spectrum from the relatively more sober to the relatively more bizarre.

For example, Neil Anderson's EMM ministry includes many good elements: digging out false beliefs, applying truth, calling for prayer, repentance, progressive sanctification, and commitment to the word of God. He can wake people up to the reality of spiritual warfare. I appreciate Anderson's pilgrimage away from "power encounters" toward "truth encounters." I also appreciate his biblical and practical criticisms of those who do power encounters. But I question his conceptualization of moral demonization and regret its prominence in his writings. And the formulaic nature of his "steps to freedom in Christ" is problematic. But God will use what is true to help people. Where prayer is sincerely offered, truth is presented in love, and there is a call to repentance, our Lord will be pleased to show his mercy.

The previous paragraphs, however, must be qualified. EMM works constructively to the degree that the person does not buy the distinctive EMM theology but acts in repentant faith. Consider Alan, a man with a persistent anger problem. He had a "demon of anger" cast out and went on a three-day spiritual high. But then he became irritated at his wife, flushed with emotion and furious thoughts, and lashed out at her with vile words. If Alan takes EMM distinctives as true he concludes, "The demons are back." Such a conclusion plunges him into an unbiblical worldview where he will not grow in true knowledge of God, the word, the Christian life, or himself. He will consign himself to superstition and formulaic prayers. Or he may cease to be a professing Christian because his understanding of the Christian faith "doesn't work" to solve his problems.

But assume Alan did not buy into EMM, even though he had an EMM-induced experience. Instead, EMM could crystallize some important truths: "I *am* in a spiritual warfare. Someone wants to rule me! My bitterness and anger is serious and I need to deal with it. I thank my faithful savior Jesus Christ for revealing this to me. God, help me to dig out the selfish cravings that sparked my outburst. I see my pride. I've sizzled when she crossed me, and then I've bullied her with anger. God, I repent of these things. Forgive me. Thank you for Jesus Christ's merciful blood for a man as selfish as I am. I need to ask my wife's forgiveness. Lord, I need your power and guidance so I can learn how to become a peacemaker, to understand my wife's point of view, to control my tone of voice, to become patient and kind." Some people come away with a classic-mode worldview despite having had an ekballistic-mode experience.

8. "WHAT ABOUT PHENOMENA OF DEMONIC MANIFESTATION?"

"But I experienced. . ." These are three of the hardest words to argue with in America today, for experience presents itself as indubitable authority. My response is rooted in experience too, for I have seen, heard, and read the things EMM advocates speak of. And I am deeply convinced that they misinterpret, misdiagnose, and sometimes even produce those experiences. Some of my comments in this section will be speculative and controversial, but the issue needs to be tackled.

I see three possible explanations for the "manifestations of the demonic" produced in EMM contexts. These are not mutually exclusive, but could play out simultaneously. These explanations can be seen as a triple strand, logically connected.

First, many of the "demonic manifestations" are produced by highly charged expectations. An atmosphere of intense expectation can produce almost anything. Counselors find what they are looking for; counselees produce what counselors are looking for. The "power of suggestion" may sound like a cheap trick, and EMM advocates typically shake their heads in dismay that anyone would say that it could explain the bizarre and powerful phenomena they have seen. But suggestion is a force of vast and subtle power. People with demonological beliefs "see and experience" demons just as people with modern beliefs "see and experience" psychopathological symptoms.

When I read the case studies and verbatim transcripts of ekballistic encounters, I see profound issues of sin that are passed over, repackaged, and projected as demon intruders. For example, many of the anecdotes stress that a person was a sincere, sweet Christian who loved the Lord and had a heart for ministry, but somehow could not shake terribly distressing lustful, angry, or depressing thoughts. EMM ministers tend to interpret unpleasant, "ego-alien" thoughts as demons. This shows a lack of true understanding of both God and the remnant sin in human nature.

The heart of darkness where the devil's voice is heard is often trivialized or passed over. It is not that EMM advocates take sin lightly; rather they do not take it deeply. This is far more than a play on words. They have taken in too many of the expectations of "the victorious Christian life" and not enough of the problem of indwelling sin. They lack a grasp of the dynamics of both sin and sanctification. Where their counselors expect to find demons, confused and struggling people will produce the expected.

Second, perhaps Satan himself cooperates with error to produce the special effects generated by EMM teaching and practice. EMM is fundamentally wrong—on biblical grounds—about the demonization of indwelling sin. The intimate wooings and brutal slavemastery of the devil do not translate into having an unclean spirit. If the EMM worldview actually embraces and teaches points of occult theology, who would be happier than the arch-liar?

One EMM teacher told the following story: "In one counseling session with Alice, I asked the demon called Non-acceptance if he had used the concept that Christians cannot be inhabited by demons. He replied, 'Oh, yes! We use it all the time. It is one of the best tools we have ever promoted.' "[7] This man believed a demon told him the truth. But perhaps the "demon" called Non-acceptance was a Satanic-fleshly production. Perhaps it deceived both Alice and the counselor into wallowing in a worldview and practices unsupported by Scripture.

Most EMM practitioners will admit that, on occasion, certain "manifestations" had the look and feel of demons but proved bogus. The names of demons are frequently absurdities—fantastical transmutations of confused flesh. Many of the "conversations with demons" reveal that the counselor is as confused as anyone else. Worse still, EMM practical theology lets experience interpret Scripture instead of letting Scripture interpret experience.

Third, EMM could actually invoke demonic activity. "Voices" in the mind are not uncommon: blasphemous mockeries, spurts of temptation to wallow in vile fantasy or behavior, persuasive lines of unbelief. Classic spiritual warfare interprets these as coming from the evil one and promises that he will flee when resisted with the armor of light.[8] It recognizes that the iniquitous human heart is the bridge between temptation and sin. But EMM calls such voices demon inhabitants attached to one's heart. EMM techniques induce people to relinquish conscious control.

Sometimes this loss of control happens through identifiable hypnotic techniques. In aggressive power encounters, an authoritarian deliverance minister can create hypnotic effects in troubled and suggestible counselees. This can happen both in public meetings and private consultations. The first power encounter I witnessed actually reminded me of speeches by Adolf Hitler I had seen on television as a youth. Hitler was a master at manipulative, hypnotic communication, at generating mass hysteria phenomena. If "voices" really do talk to us, then hypnotic techniques may actually encourage mediumistic outbreaks by inviting the person to step aside.

These outbreaks do not only happen in power encounters. Less dramatic deliverance ministers directly invite the counselee to relax, relinquish control, and let the voices speak through them. This form of suggestion is no less mediumistic and manipulative. The manifestation phenomena could well be an artifact of the worldview and techniques. Contrary to biblical example, contemporary "manifestations" typically occur in contexts charged with emotion and expectation where the pump is primed with EMM teaching.

Something of uncanny evil seems to happen in some EMM encounters. Perhaps the practitioners are—naively—actually contributing to the production of bizarre evil. When instead we address people as people, recognizing that they are in a spiritual warfare, we will remain on biblical ground.

This chapter has shown that EMM distinctives are wrong not only in the broad strokes, but also in the details. We have seen that EMM views and practices are unsupportable biblically. We *are* in a warfare. But we need to understand and fight that warfare the way God intends.

10

A BETTER WAY

HOW DO WE DEAL WITH "HARD CASES" and people who are stuck?
How do we help non-Christians who are spiritually afflicted?
How do we help a professing Christian who struggles in bondage
to sin and misery? How, in short, do we fight spiritual warfare
biblically and effectively? Robust biblical counseling—the ministry of prayer and the word in love—cuts deep and is highly
practical, as this chapter will show.

To show how more classic biblical counseling works we will
look at two case studies.[1] These are longer than those in most
books because "snapshot" cases too easily communicate false
impressions. Classic spiritual warfare is detailed, bringing deeds of
care and words of light into the particulars of an individual's life.
Neither case involves a sophisticated practitioner of EMM, nor
could they be considered "typical" of EMM recipients, for there
is no typical. But these cases capture real-life problems and provide a stage on which to view certain key features in the call to
reclaim spiritual warfare.

ALLISON'S ASSAILANTS

Allison is a thirty-four-year-old single woman who has become
involved in EMM ministry over the past five years. She came
to Christ in her mid-twenties, out of a background that included
some witchcraft and lesbianism. She felt that she had experi-

enced deliverance from demons through EMM when she renounced occultism and immorality. Allison has never felt any tug back into those lifestyles and is grateful to the Lord. She wants to help deliver other people. She works as a receptionist in a dental office, but her real interest is to serve God through extensive volunteer ministry.

After we spent several hours talking back and forth about EMM, she opened up in a more personal vein. "Let me be frank. I see that the real battle is for my own mind. Most of my deliverance is with me. I'm not a devil doctor; I'm not out to exorcise people; I'm not on a power trip. I really use deliverance most often on myself. Lies and feelings come in straight from the devil. I need to use spiritual warfare to protect and deliver myself. I rebuke and drive away the demons that harass, tempt, and try to enslave me."

She gave an example of blasphemous thoughts that intruded, calling them unpleasant and unwelcome mental visitors. She told how she would take authority over these demons in Jesus' name, sending them to the pit. She also described irrational anger that would well up in her mind in the form of demons. She said, "I deal with these like bubbles in a glass of Coke. They bubble up into my mind and have to be waved on through. I love the Lord with all my heart, and this anger just isn't me. I'm thankful for all God has done. So I rebuke the demons of anger. I cancel their ground. I bind and cast them out. I don't like those intrusive angry thoughts. I'm committed to *not* thinking those things. They're an ugly, evil attack. I just try to blow them on through."

Allison describes—with her own wrinkles—an ekballistic method for working out personal problems, assaults, struggles, and temptations. She calls this "spiritual warfare." What should we make of what she says? We have seen—for example in James 4 and Ephesians 4—that anger *is* intimately connected with the devil. And in one sense, because every sin is connected with Satan, every problem is a devil problem. But has she understood

herself and her life situation accurately? Is it right to resort to *NO!*
an ekballistic method of ministry for purposes of sanctification?

As we talked further she reiterated, with some vehemence,
"These thoughts are alien thoughts. They aren't me. I'm not
really an angry person—I love the Lord. These thoughts are
inner opposition. They contradict my position as a blood-bought,
Spirit-filled child of God, and I know and feel their contradiction
and lies. I need the Lord's protection and power to deliver me
from these demons of blasphemy and anger."

Allison's entire story was moving but troubling. On the one
hand, it squares with many versions of EMM orthodoxy. She
had been discipled intensively in this method for living the
Christian life and fighting life's battles. On the other hand, her
framework for understanding life did not square with anything
recognizably biblical. No psalm, no prophet, no gospel, no epistle communicated her sort of vision. Her zeal was admirable; her
faith and gratitude to Christ seemed genuine, but her worldview
was disturbingly unbiblical.

As we talked I put forward to her some different approaches
to anger.[2] "Instead of blowing the bubbles through or binding
the demons, why don't you just stop? Maybe there's more going
on than you're allowing. Collect your wits. Ask God for wisdom—he's able to protect his lambs. And then as you hold the
anger in view for a minute, ask yourself some questions.

"First, locate the anger. Maybe it popped up in a vacuum,
but that's not usually true. When did you start to get angry?
What was going on at the time? What happened? Unless you
stop and look at what you are reacting to, how can you start to
sort through how God would have you respond?

"Second, stop and look at the exact form your anger takes.
What are you thinking? What are you tempted to do? What are
you feeling? Who is the target of your anger? It is worth knowing
if your anger is at God, another person, a traffic jam, or at yourself. Dig into the experience a minute. Your Father won't plunge
you into an abyss for stopping to sort out what's happening.

"Third, know that God is interested in renewing your heart. James 1:14–15 says that your sins—and anger is one of the major sins—come from your cravings. What did you want? Or did you fear something? What was it? What particular beliefs were motoring inside your anger? Was there something you craved at the moment the impulse to anger manifested? Instead of just calling the angry thoughts and feelings a demonic insertion, ask what lies the real devil may have you believing that produce anger.

"Fourth, stop and consider who God is and what he says. Remember what is true and who your armor is in the heat of battle! What does it mean that God is in control of your situation, that he is bigger even than the devil's temptations? What does it mean that God is holy, that his commands to love expose your anger and your cravings? What does it mean that Jesus loves you, forgives you, helps you? Your Shepherd can give you courage to stop and look. He will help you learn to trust God and act in love no matter what is happening to you. What does it mean that your Father is a Vinedresser who prunes those he loves? What is he pruning when angry thoughts bubble up in you? Seize the bubble that you might know both your own heart and your God better, so you can change and become more fruitful.

"Fifth, now that you have caught fresh glimpses of yourself and God, ask how you need to meet God. Where do you need mercy and grace to help in your time of need? He is your refuge—you don't need to fear. How can you seek and find the Searcher and Knower of hearts who is faithful and true in love for his children? Ask for forgiveness and help. Anger is a tough battle. It makes us like the devil. But God is willing to be found. Pray fervently—and intelligently—in light of the real battle we have been getting to know.

"Sixth, ask how God wants you to change. How does he want you to think about and tackle your situation? Let's get down to practical details. What will change look like in the situations that provoke anger?"

After exploring the answers to these classic-mode sanctification questions, it became clear that the supposed demons of anger appeared in certain definable circumstances and not in others. For instance, intrusive angry thoughts appeared when Allison had trouble forgiving a partner in ministry whom she felt snubbed her and looked down on her. She wanted to forgive and love that person, according to Christ's command, but she reacted against him. The man in question seemed to have a streak of arrogance. Allison wanted his approval and recognition. She also had fantasies that he might become her husband, though he evidenced no interest. He dated women who were all five to ten years younger than Allison.

Angry thoughts would also intrude on Friday or Saturday nights when Allison wasn't out ministering and stayed home alone. Sometimes her anger targeted the man who had spurned her. Other times it pointed at herself for "messing up my life before I was a Christian, and now I'm thirty-four, look kind of beat up by life, and don't have a chance at getting married." These reactions frightened and discouraged her. She looked to Jesus and ekballistics for a simple fix.

Sometimes God himself was the object of her blasphemous anger, although she barely dared to admit this. But when she craved recognition, a husband, an ease for loneliness, she felt that God also let her down. It is not difficult to find the God-substitutes in people who are angry at God. Allison's "irrational" bouts of anger—and self-accusation and self-pity—did not fit her theology of herself; her theology of assailing demons mapped onto these experiences. In response she resorted to EMM.

Allison's temptations to anger, however, are explained far better within the Bible's worldview. Cravings of the flesh collide with recalcitrant reality and anger streams forth. The devil's malice took her coworker's arrogance and lack of romantic interest, and conspired to plunge Allison into anger and despair. The devil would make Allison like himself. But her heavenly Father was simultaneously working in and through the same situation to renew her confused soul. He intended to transform her, inside and out, through the truth. Certain cravings and lies interfered with simple love for God.[3]

The classic mode of spiritual warfare—set in the coherent wisdom of the biblical worldview—made sense of Allison's real-life struggles. She began to understand herself, God, and her warfare in a completely new way. The questions I posed were not magical; they simply located a real person's real struggles in the real world that God works within. The questions that organized my conversations with Allison were these: What is the situation? What is the sinful reaction? What is the sinful motive? How does God speak and act in this situation? What is the new motive? And finally, what is the new response?

Truth set her in a context of realistic hope. It gave her a direction to walk in by which her mind could be renewed through obedience. It spoke wisdom to renew her actions, hopes, emotional reactions, priorities, and the structure of her conscience. It sent the devil—with his temptations, lies, confusions, and accusations—packing.

Sadly, the EMM worldview had already shortcircuited knowledge of God and herself. Ironically, as time went on, it was even derailing knowledge of the devil. The Bible never addresses Satan in and of himself but only as he exists and acts with respect to God and people. To misconstrue God and people is inevitably to misconstrue the enemy. The classic biblical worldview replaces a warrior's confused zeal with a warrior who is becoming wise. Allison had been living in a cartoon world—a depthless caricature of reality. God's truth brought her into a reality with depth, detail, and many other good things, including the freedom in Christ to mature as a redeemed human being.

BOB AND HIS DEMON

Bob is a forty-two-year-old married man with four children—all girls, ages thirteen, ten, eight, and six. He is tormented by what he believes is a demon of lust. He feels almost powerless against it. In his experience, this demon woos, incites, inflames, enslaves, and leads him as if he had a ring in his nose. Then it mocks and accuses him after he falls. Bob described the "video store" of his mind with its "Adults Only" section. Behind the closed door of this "stronghold" he has accumulated his "tape collection." This collection of fantasies was built up from experiences with former girlfriends, voyeuristic incidents, pornography, and his own creative imagination. "A dragon lives inside me, in that room. When I open that door I become the dragon. I'm lustful, I'm proud, I'm the king who commands sex. Then each time after it happens the dragon turns and accuses me, and I'm the miserable and disgusting slave who's blown it again."

Bob's marriage to Jane is often rocky. He is frequently preoccupied with his inner struggles, and presents a face to the family of brooding, depression, irritability, ennui, or demandingness. Jane has glimpses of the problems he struggles with, but he keeps much of it to himself. She knows neither the intensity nor the frequency of his struggles with lust and despair. But she does know that she cannot stand—or understand—the overflow of negative emotion and selfish actions that come her way from Bob. Their sexual relationship is sporadic, averaging every couple of weeks but with many oscillations, such as two to three times within a day and then nothing for a month. Neither finds sexual relations to be emotionally intimate.

Bob and Jane bicker and sometimes blow up at each other. They do not repent, forgive, and reconcile very well after tense times. They sometimes mutter a subdued "I'm sorry, I didn't mean to hurt you," when guilt gets the better of them. But the agitants, irritants, and depressants to their relationship inevitably surface again soon. Neither contemplates divorce, because they believe that would be wrong, but their marriage seems a hopeless stalemate.

Bob sells industrial machinery, operating on straight commission basis. It is a feast or famine business. When doing well he is free and easy with money: trips to Disneyworld, weekend ski trips, a home entertainment center, generous commitments to his church and its missionaries, a lawn service. But when things are tight, pressure mounts everywhere: credit-card debt rises; charitable commitments go by the boards—with much guilt; the emotional life within the family becomes strained. Bob has gotten in trouble with the IRS for failing to pay taxes and is slowly making headway on a repayment schedule. He puts in long hours at work and is preoccupied outside of work. Bob and Jane have never set money aside for lean times or toward retirement.

Twice Bob was put on probation by his boss for filing false reports of sales calls to clients. But because he is an effective salesman, his boss wants to keep him—and keep him in line. The secretaries who handle Bob's correspondence and type his proposals describe him as a "beast"—or worse—to work for. He is erratic, rushes in at the last minute, and expects it to be done yesterday. He throws tantrums or flirts in order to elevate his work to the top of the stack.

When Bob was in college he accepted the Lord; he is intensely committed to him. He and his family attend a Bible-believing church with charismatic leanings. His sense of God is intense with "feelings and leadings" studding his conversation, but with a core of more objective conviction. Jane too is a committed Christian. She roughly agrees with Bob theologically, though both of them tend to see Jane as the "practical" one and Bob as the "spiritual" one. Each alternately feels either inferior or superior to the other, depending on whether practicality or spirituality is the needed commodity in the current situation.

Bob has no close friends. He can be congenial and humorous when in public or when meeting new people. He can be very "spiritual" in church gatherings, and feels deep religious feelings: joy in worship, impressions of what the Lord is saying in particular situations, burdens for prayer. He thinks he may receive a "word of knowledge" regarding what gifts other people have. "But my sin and bondage and guilt keep me from serving the Lord the way I could."

Regarding Bob's background, he was raised Roman Catholic and had a superstitious mother. She set up a small shrine in the corner of the dining room with crucifixes, statuettes, and medallions of saints, candles, and other holy objects. She would periodically visit a medium. Bob's mother was particularly fearful of her children becoming ill and would give them protective medallions as she directed the medium to enlist spirit forces to watch over her kids. Bob describes his father as demanding and having occasional outbursts of temper. His father beat Bob's mother and the kids in drunken rages when Bob was preschool age. But after the worst incident—the police had intervened—his father straightened out. Bob has no memories of his father either drunk or violent, but learned of this in adulthood from his older sister.

Bob has struggled with immorality since his teens. He was a playboy and partied heavily during his last two years of high school and first two years at community college. He figures that a particularly stubborn demon used this time to gain a foothold in his life. After coming to Christ the flagrant immorality ceased, but the ogling, pornography, and mental tapes continued. He went to Bible school for a semester after college, thinking the Lord might be calling him to "full-time ministry." Bob dropped out, however, because his conscience was troubled by lust and he needed to make money after he and Jane got married. They had met the first week of Bible school; two months later they were engaged. Shortly thereafter she became pregnant, and they quickly married. She miscarried the child a month later.

Bob deals with his lust and other problems through prayer, fasting, and taking authority over evil powers. He claims ground and then binds and rebukes demons. He believes he had four demons—Lust, Anger, Uncleanness, and Pride—cast out of him in spectacular fashion about ten years ago by a popular deliverance minister. The lust problem had gotten bad when Jane was in the last few months of pregnancy. Bob thinks that Lust must have reentered when he again dabbled in pornography a few weeks later. He wonders if Self-Accusation may have come in with Lust. He also wonders if he inherited an Occult Power demon that has lurked in his mind all these years. Maybe the initial deliverance only cleaned out the sentries but left the master of the stronghold in place—partially hindered but still able to work much of his will.

Bob prays "warfare prayers," claims promises from the Bible, and considers revisiting a deliverance minister. His reading of the Bible is utterly fragmented. He rarely reads even a chapter of the Bible straight through. Rather he lifts verses from here and there, usually out of context. His working theology is a mishmash of truths, partial truths, and errors with huge gaps and equally huge alien insertions.

Many people look up to Bob in his church. My case study has highlighted the darkness in his life, but his faith and enthusiasm can be effervescent. He can be extremely generous and sacrificial with time and money—if somewhat impulsive and erratic. He was recently asked to help with the College & Career group, but quit after a month because of his battle with lust toward the young women. Nobody is close enough to Bob to know that this was the issue, and people took at face value his begging off with the excuse of "too much pressure at work right now." His church relationships are sealed off from what he really struggles with: "I'd be too ashamed. And my failures would discourage the faith of the younger adults who look up to me."

Sexual fantasy and food—Bob's other vice—are release valves from his sense of failure and frustration, as well as contributors to his sense of failure. When he is not fasting, Bob will often "pig out," and it shows on his 5'7" 220-pound frame. Does he have a demon of Gluttony? At times he is bitter at God because "I fast and pray in private to my heavenly Father, just like Matthew 6 says, and God doesn't work." But Bob also has a buoyant spirit. He loves God and believes that God's mercies are new every morning.

Bob's working theology looks something like this: "Step out of line or stop living by faith and you're in big trouble. God has saved us by the blood of his beloved Son, and his mercies are new every morning, but God is not going to force anyone to believe and obey. He's provided it all, but it's up to us to claim our inheritance. We've got to make the positive confession or we lose it." He views Satan as wielding a tremendous amount of power as "the god of this world." Satan's minions can freely access his mind, read and invade his thought life, and engineer circumstances to enslave him. Prayer, fasting, and spiritual warfare—EMM style—are his only protection in this chancy world where he is caught between a beckoning God up there and an active Satan down here. Satan apparently has more raw power than God to affect our lives, although when Bob gets in touch with God he always has the victory. "The Lord invites us, but we have to believe, come, eat, and drink, as Jesus says in John 6."

What should we make of Bob? He has all the much-cited ingredients to assume inhabiting demons: a mother with occult leanings; childhood abuse; his own entrenched anger, lust, and gluttony; intense self-recrimination; a belief system that expects unclean spirits of sin. EMM theory would say that there is a high likelihood of Bob being demonized. An EMM practitioner could have brought about a "demon manifestation" in Bob because the pump was primed. He was distressed, confused, emotionally unstable, ready to believe demonological explanations, and eager for ekballistic solutions.

But Bob was *not* demonized; once again the biblical account is wiser and more effective. Scripture says Bob is foolish and immature, describing him as a captive of the devil to do his will—a matter of basic sin. Bob has been a Christian for some twenty years but has learned few of the rudiments of the faith and too many of the distortions of superstitious spirituality. Advocates of both EMM and classic warfare would agree that Bob is seriously confused. EMM proponents would say that he distorts a fundamentally sound paradigm and needs to be taught to make it work for him. But as a follower of the classic way, I think he expresses some logical extensions of a fundamentally unsound paradigm. He needs a different paradigm.

There is no complexity in Bob's life that demands recourse to the ekballistic—or the therapeutic, for that matter. Bob has garden-variety problems, albeit writ large, deeply entrenched, complicated by much confusion and faulty belief, and established over many years. Bob must learn to fight spiritual warfare so that he might grow in grace and become a mature man of God.

TWELVE STEPS TO A FAR MORE POWERFUL WAY

Let me close with a series of counsels to Bob that provide a sampler of the weapons of war. As we have seen throughout the book, the situation is the opposite of what we are led to expect. The heavy artillery is not ekballistic fireworks; rather, a series of countless "small" changes and choices is far more explosive and life-changing. When multifaceted truth encounters moral slavery with the truth and power of God, the result is a far more powerful way of spiritual warfare.

First, Bob must fight and win spiritual warfare through discovering the Creator God who rules heaven and earth. He cannot fight an enemy whom he invests with many of God's powers. He needs to understand how the universe really works, disentangling the many lies he believes and obeys.[4]

Second, Bob must fight and win spiritual warfare through learning to find refuge in the Lord Jesus Christ. His nervous heroics of "taking authority" bear little resemblance to the confidence of knowing the Shepherd of souls. The "name and the blood" that Bob has so often claimed need to become realities believed and known rather than magic words. Too much of his warfare depends on his own "spiritual" efforts, rather than on God's promises of the effective love of Christ.[5]

Third, Bob must fight and win spiritual warfare through learning to dig into the Scripture in search of true wisdom. He has treated Bible verses as magic charms rather than as the coherent word of the coherent God who is to be feared and obeyed. Careful listeners become wise, and wise people stand on the evil day.[6]

Fourth, Bob must fight and win spiritual warfare through stopping fighting alone. He needs friends to love him, know him, pray for him, counsel him, and hold him accountable. The dragon in the back room can intimidate an isolated individual, but must fall before a platoon.[7]

Fifth, Bob must fight and win spiritual warfare through growing to understand the thoughts and intentions of his heart. Numerous specific false beliefs and deceptive cravings bend his life toward darkness. Jesus Christ promises aid to those who learn what they really need help with.[8] The metaphorical "dragon" attracts a lot of his attention. But how about the "playing God" in his mental fantasy world? How about the frustrated lusts for money and human approval that generate pressure, setting him up to find sexual lust an attractive escape?[9] The real dragon has a thousand disguises and deceits. The Savior has a new identity that can replace the old.

Sixth, Bob must fight and win spiritual warfare through speaking words that do genuine good to Jane and others. When he is patient, kind, forbearing, forgiving, candid, constructive, judicious, and peaceable the devil will flee. Bob's blustering, chaotic, aimless, impulsive speech tips off his folly. The wise tongue repels the liar and murderer.[10]

Seventh, Bob must fight and win spiritual warfare through entering into Jane's life—and letting her enter his life—both for seasons of honest prayer and to delight in sexual love within their marriage. She can become his ally on many levels. What a surprising God who includes sexual joy in his manual of war![11]

Eighth, Bob must fight and win spiritual warfare through giving his boss an honest day's work and treating his secretary with respect. In other words, through loving his neighbor in the work place. The outcome of the battle hinges on a thousand skirmishes and hand-to-hand combats. A man with integrity in the workplace will be a man in whom the dragons are dying.[12]

Ninth, Bob must fight and win spiritual warfare through paying his taxes and handling money wisely. Those who are faithful in a little thing are faithful in much. The sloppy folly of Bob's life expresses itself in countless little defeats. Sometimes the first victories of wisdom come in areas remote from the "felt-dragon."[13]

Tenth, Bob must fight and win spiritual warfare through driving his car at a speed so he does not need to brake when he sees a police cruiser with a radar gun. Satan glories in those who follow their lusts and despise authority.[14] God will have glory when an unbridled lifestyle comes under reins.

Eleventh, Bob must fight and win spiritual warfare through learning to aim his heart at what true prayer intends. The battle turns on whether Bob will aim to glorify God, obey him, rely on him, submit his need to him, seek aid, and repent of sin, praying:

Our Father, who art in heaven,
Hallowed be thy Name.
Thy kingdom come,
Thy will be done, on earth as it is in heaven.
Give us this day our daily bread.
And forgive us our trespasses, as we forgive those who trespass
    against us.
And lead us not into temptation, but deliver us from evil.
For thine is the kingdom, and the power, and the glory, for
    ever and ever. Amen.

This way of praying enters reality and replaces the confused and ritualistic prayers Bob has prayed.

And twelfth, Bob must fight and win spiritual warfare through not giving in to well-cultivated sexual lusts. This is no different in principle from any other area of this battle. EMM advocates are right that sexual lust and anger are particularly tough sins to break. Scripture has always indicated that, as it mentions and discusses these sins countless times. But tough battles do not point to demonization. They point to the Lord Jesus as the Savior from our sins.[15]

Bob's reaction as we talked through these things was fascinating. He literally shook his head and rubbed his eyes like a man waking up from sleep. "I *know* these things," he said. "How could I have forgotten?"

Bob was right. Satan is the sleep inducer, the one who labors to make us drunk, blind, deaf, benighted, and forgetful. Classic warfare may not seem heroic at a first glance. But what begins as "small things" can rearrange our lives forever and bring God vast glory. After all, the only thing Job did was refrain from cursing, but the impact of his patience in affliction was incalculable—to God's glory, our well being, and Satan's humiliation.

What was the outcome of the story? It was as if God handed Bob a number of small "laboratories" for working out what it meant to walk in the light. How would he treat his secretary? Would he view events as within his loving Father's sovereignty? Would he obey the speed limit? Establish honest accountability to friends? Engage in more systematic Bible study? Believe that Jesus loved him? Cherish Jane during sexual relations, and let her know how to pray for him? Focus his prayers on the real issues where he needed help? Bob started to grow in purity for the first time since he had made his break with serial fornication years before.

The result was that Bob's impoverished world of semi-occult "warfare" became a rich world of true warfare. The human being came center stage and took up the task assigned by his Creator and Savior. The world, the flesh, and the devil were each given their proper proportion and role. The details of life became significant. And God in Christ by the Spirit's power and word appeared on the stage of life with a relevance that astonished Bob. He began to see all of life before the face of almighty God. And Bob learned *how* to grow in grace for the first time. In short, Bob was changed forever by learning to change day by day.

Martin Luther put this way the lessons Bob learned:

This life, therefore, is not righteousness
    but growth in righteousness,
not health but healing,
not being but becoming,
not rest but exercise.
We are not yet what we shall be but we are growing toward it;
    the process is not yet finished but it is going on;
This is not the end but it is the road;
    all does not yet gleam in glory but all is being purified.[16]

Reclaiming spiritual warfare means learning afresh how God pursues his glory in our lives. It means gaining an understanding of progressive sanctification in a Christian culture habituated to look for quick fixes. It means learning to see heroic dramas played out in tiny corners of life. It means becoming human, renewed in the image of Jesus Christ—the pioneer and perfecter of faith. It means learning how to become Christians.

All the surface appeal and short-term attraction is on the side of power encounters with demonic agents. Excitement, drama, the promise of all-out confrontation, and complete supernatural change—power encounters have them all. Engaging evil with truth, by contrast, seems dry, weak, dull, old-fashioned, and unspiritual. But surprise is always at the heart of the gospel. As in the birth, life, death, and resurrection of the country Galilean, so in spiritual warfare today: strength is subverted by weakness, worldly wisdom by truth, riches by poverty—and the powers of darkness are best felled by the small, weak words and works of faith and obedience.

Sola Deo Gloria.

NOTES

Chapter 1: Reclaiming Spiritual Warfare

1. The case studies I cite throughout the book are altered in all identifying details and frequently are composites.
2. See Frank E. Peretti, *This Present Darkness* (Wheaton, Ill.: Crossway, 1986) and *Piercing the Darkness* (Wheaton, Ill.: Crossway, 1989).
3. And its relatives, *praos, prautees, praus.*
4. See Ephesians 4:12–16.
5. Scripture abounds with lists characterizing those who live outside the kingdom of light. The lengthiest descriptions are found in Mark 7:20–23, Romans 1:18–32, 1 Corinthians 6:9–10, Galatians 5:19–21, 2 Timothy 3:1–5, and Revelation 21:8.
6. See Acts 26:18.

Chapter 2: What Is Spiritual Warfare?

1. See Neil T. Anderson, *The Bondage Breaker* (Eugene, Oreg: Harvest House, 1990); Timothy M. Warner, *Spiritual Warfare: Victory over the Powers of This Dark World* (Wheaton, Ill.: Crossway, 1991); Tom White, *The Believer's Guide to Spiritual Warfare* (Ann Arbor, Mich.: Servant, 1990) and *Breaking Strongholds: How Spiritual Warfare Sets Captives Free* (Ann Arbor, Mich.: Servant, 1993); Ed Murphy, *The Handbook for Spiritual Warfare* (Nashville, Tenn.: Thomas Nelson, 1992).
2. The psychological/psychiatric strand plays a prominent role, for example, in Dickason, Anderson, Murphy, and in James Friesen's

writing on Multiple Personality Disorder. See Friesen, *Uncovering the Mystery of MPD* (San Bernandino Calif.: Here's Life Publications, 1991).

3. See Ray Stedman, *Spiritual Warfare: Winning the Daily Battle with Satan* (Portland, Oreg.: Multnomah, 1975); Jay E. Adams, *The War Within: A Biblical Strategy for Spiritual Warfare* (Eugene, Oreg.: Harvest House, 1989); John MacArthur, *How to Meet the Enemy* (Wheaton, Ill.: Victor Books, 1992).

4. Frederick S. Leahy, *Satan Cast Out: A Study in Biblical Demonology* (Great Britain: Banner of Truth Trust, 1975), p. 8. I recommend Leahy's careful biblical, theological, and historical work to the reader who wants to study the wider issues of practical demonology.

Chapter 3: Ask Questions of the Text in Context

1. See Deuteronomy 29:29—what God has chosen to reveal completely fulfills his purpose.

2. See Proverbs 2:1–10.

3. In fact, Ephesians 6:10–20 develops themes taught throughout the letter. Our deliverance from the power of the devil has already been described generally in 2:1–10 (see 2:2 for mention of the enemy), and more specifically in 4:15–32 (and throughout chapters 5 and 6; see 4:27 for mention of the enemy). The entire book of Ephesians is a primer in classic-mode spiritual warfare without a hint of EMM.

Chapter 4: Cultures Dark with the Occult

1. See Ephesians 2:12.

2. See 2 Chronicles 33:2–7.

3. Judges 17–21 portrays this sort of world, and is perhaps the low point of the Old Testament. It sets the stage for the revelation of the anointed king.

4. John Bunyan's *Holy War* identifies the "eargate" as the crucial point of battle for the loyalty of the town of "Mansoul."

5. King Saul initially was very pleased with David (1 Samuel 16:21–22). But when the people began to praise David more than their king, Saul's attitude turned to anger, suspicion, and fear (1 Samuel 18:6–9, 12). Twice when the evil spirit from God

came upon Saul, and while David played his harp, Saul attempted to kill him (1 Samuel 18:10–11; 19:9). Saul did not have demons of anger and suspicion; he was angry and suspicious.

6. Compare the appearance of Moses and Elijah in Matthew 17:3, where the purpose was to reveal the glory of the Messiah.

7. Judges 9:23–24 similarly shows God using an evil spirit to stir up trouble in order to serve his purposes in judgment.

8. Satan requested to touch Job's "bone and flesh." This was a two-pronged request, as the story makes clear. First, Job's body was wracked with disease. Then the "bone of [his] bones and flesh of [his] flesh" (Genesis 2:23) directly counseled him to curse God.

9. See Isaiah 53:6; Psalms 51, 103, 131; Ephesians 4–6; 1 Timothy 1:15.

Chapter 5: Sin and Suffering

1. The first ten chapters of the Gospel of Mark particularly highlight Jesus casting out demons and healing.

2. See Habakkuk 1:13; James 1:13; 1 John 1:5.

3. See 1 John 3.

4. See Romans 6:23.

5. See 1 Kings 22; 1 Timothy 4:1; 1 John 4:1–6.

6. Matthew 4:23–25 and many other statements make this link explicitly: for example, Luke 6:18; 7:21; 8:2; 9:42; 13:11–13.

7. The same Greek word—peirasmos—means both "trials" and "temptation," for situational trials typically tempt us to moral evil.

8. See Matthew 4:1–11; Luke 4:1–13.

9. Notice that there is no ekballistic response to Satan's moral influence on Peter. Similarly, when Satan later requested to sift Peter like wheat, Jesus' response was in the classic mode: prayer, teaching, warning, promises, patient restoration.

10. Those who want to follow these ideas further will notice that the pattern we traced in Mark 7–8 is replicated throughout the gospels and Acts. Jesus juxtaposes miracles (aiming at situational evil and revealing his goodness) with teaching, reproof, preaching, and questioning (aiming at moral evil and challenging our badness).

11. Of course, *our* trusting in God usually entails turning *from* something evil—something Jesus never had to do. See Acts 26:18.

Chapter 6: Jesus' Mode of Ministry and Ours

1. See Matthew 17:24–27.
2. See Matthew 22:16–22; Romans 13:1–7.
3. See Luke 5:4; John 21:3–6.
4. See Matthew 14:24–33.
5. See John 13:29.
6. See Acts 20:34 and the following.
7. This statement would be on personal authority if we meant, "Repent to me, or I will kill you."
8. In some circumstances—with his disciples or the crowds—Jesus models our way of confronting sin. In others—to the barren fig tree—he acts in the power mode of ultimate judgment.
9. Luke 7:14; Luke 8:54; John 11:43.
10. See Psalms 29, 104, 147.
11. Mark 4:35–41. See also Matthew 8:23–27.
12. 1 Kings 18:42; see also 18:36–37.
13. Does this mean that demons are not malicious agents of temptation or false teaching intended to plunge people into bondage to sin? Of course not. The Bible speaks of those who "follow deceiving spirits and things taught by demons" (1 Timothy 4:1). But in this context, Paul places his emphasis on the *content*—of the teaching and the false teachers. One resists such demonically inspired lies by resisting the message and messenger and holding fast to truth. As we have seen repeatedly, EMM is uncalled for with moral evil.
14. See, for example, the summary statement in Matthew 4:23–24 and a specific incident in Matthew 12:22.
15. Psalm 103:3–4; Isaiah 61:1, 2.

Chapter 7: A Host of Further Questions

1. See Acts 2:22.
2. Other similar passages speak of the first wave of apostles and disciples (Acts 5:12; 15:12; 2 Corinthians 12:12) as if they were

instruments of the works of Jesus himself (Acts 14:3; Romans 15:15–20; Hebrews 2:3–4).

3. C. Fred Dickason, *Demon Possession and the Christian* (Chicago: Moody Press, 1987).

4. Notice how Acts 8:14 pointedly fulfills Acts 1:8. The interpretive center of the passage is "Samaria had accepted the word of God."

5. What follows must be qualified with a tentativeness appropriate to drawing general principles from a narrative. Obviously, Acts 8 is not a handbook on "how to deal with people from an occult past." Rather it is a story of what happened to one person from an occult past who happened to be present when the promise of the Spirit began spreading to people outside Jerusalem.

6. From my observations, lust for power is one of several characteristic reasons people pursue the occult. Other reasons include terror of spiritual forces, a craving to understand and control life circumstances, lusts for esoteric knowledge and experience, lust for money, and desires to intimidate, control, and awe others. Several of these seem to be present in Simon.

7. See Thessalonians 1:9, 1 Peter 4:3, and the discussion in Acts 15 about what to do with these idolaters who were coming to Christ.

8. John Calvin, *A Harmony of the Gospels Matthew, Mark and Luke*, vol. II (Grand Rapids, Mich.: Eerdmans, 1972), pp. 53–54.

9. See Luke 8:12, 15.

10. See John 13:2; Acts 5:3.

11. See John 13:27; Luke 22:3; John 6:70; John 17:12.

12. See Acts 26:18.

13. See 2 Corinthians 4:3–6.

14. See Ephesians 2:2–10.

15. See 2 Timothy 2:25–26.

16. See, for instance, Romans 1 and 6, Galatians 5.

Chapter 8: "Resist the Devil"

1. EMM advocates frequently import a demonological understanding of spiritual warfare and ekballistic practices into such passages as Ephesians 6:10–20, James 4:6, and 1 Peter 5:8, which we will look at more closely below. Only 1 Corinthians 12:9–10, 28–30 possibly alludes to ekballistic ministry. It

contains three references to a gift of "workings of power," which could well refer to driving out demons, for it is a standard way to refer to the powerful effects of EMM and other power modes. The close pairing with "gifts of healings" reinforces the notion that Paul may be referring to healing the demon-afflicted. If so, this is the only reference to ministry to those who suffer from demons outside of Matthew, Mark, Luke, and Acts. But it focuses on how to keep proper perspective and priorities in the midst of dramatic mercy ministries.

2. I will use epistles as shorthand for both the epistles and Revelation.
3. See 1 Corinthians 5:5 and 1 Timothy 1:20.
4. See Numbers 33:55 for "thorn in the flesh"; see 2 Corinthians 11:13–15 for Satan's servants.
5. The epistles most commonly describe the devil in his role as liar and deceiver seeking hegemony over our beliefs and practices. See 1 John 4:1–5, Romans 16:17–20, 2 Timothy 2:26, 1 Timothy 4:1–7, 2 Corinthians 11:3–15, and 2 Corinthians 6:14–7:1.
6. See Ephesians 2:1–3, 4:17–19, 22; Ecclesiastes 9:3, and Genesis 6:5.
7. The word *anthistemi*, to resist, literally means to "stand against." Paul issues a repeated call to "stand," "stand against," and "wrestle against" in 6:11–14.
8. See also Isaiah 11:1–5.
9. See also Isaiah 59:9–21.
10. See also Isaiah 52–53—and even 40–66—on the "comfort" of Israel from sin's penalty and power through the Lord and his Servant.
11. See Genesis 15:1 and countless Psalms. Psalms 64 and 91 are particularly rich on how God, our shield, protects us from arrows. Most Christians, however, envision faith itself as the shield rather than God as the shield behind which faith takes refuge.
12. See also Isaiah 59:9–21.
13. See also Isaiah 49:1–7. There is perhaps an overtone of Isaiah 11:4 as well.
14. The book of Revelation has a similar focus on Satan's murderous persecutions.
15. See Psalm 22:13, 22.
16. See Psalms 7:2, 10:9, 17:12, 35:17, 57:4, and 58:6.

17. Satan's congruence with the fallen human heart operates in every passage that deals with moral evil. See Ephesians, 1 Peter, 1 Timothy 3:6, 1 Corinthians 10:6–22, and 1 John 3:1–10 and 5:16–21.
18. James 5:11 perhaps makes a remote allusion to Satan's hand in suffering, but the stress is on the sovereign goodness of God.
19. The true wisdom given freely from above (3:15, 17) flags a central theme in James. See also 1:5, 1:17–18, 4:6, 4:10, and 5:11.

Chapter 9: Rethinking the Details

1. Several popular EMM authors have written that people who question the validity of ekballistic spiritual warfare are deceived by demons (Dickason, *Demon Possession and the Christian*, pp. 191, 211) or even inhabited by demons (Pat Brooks, *Out! In the Name of Jesus* [Carol Stream, Ill.: Creation House, 1972]).
2. I trust that my own stumblings in this book also occur next to brisk steps in the right direction!
3. A legion was a unit of several thousand soldiers. In effect the demon answered Jesus, "There's an army of us inside."
4. Dickason, *Demon Possession and the Christian*, p. 221. Emphasis his.
5. See also 2 Corinthians 2:11 in context.
6. Summaries of techniques for self-deliverance can be found in Don Basham, *Deliver Us From Evil* (Old Tappan, N.J.: Fleming H. Revell, 1972); Mark I. Bubeck, *The Adversary: The Christian Versus Demon Activity* (Chicago: Moody Press, 1975), chapter 17, 4; and Anderson, *The Bondage Breaker*, chapter 12.
7. Dickason, *Demon Possession and the Christian*, p. 191.
8. This is the greatest strength of Thomas Brooks's classic, originally published in 1652, *Precious Remedies Against Satan's Devices* (Great Britain: Banner of Truth Trust, 1984).

Chapter 10: A Better Way

1. These cases are each composites from several different people. The themes are true to life, although all details have been fictionalized.

2. The next paragraphs are not verbatim, but summarize my side of a typical dialogue.
3. The three levels of Job's story reappear in endless variations. Human beings treat us wrong and circumstances are tough. Satan intends to use this to provoke us to sin. God uses it to purify our sins.
4. See Romans 8:28–29; Genesis 50:20; Job 1–2.
5. See Psalm 23; Psalm 36.
6. See Proverbs 2:1–6; Proverbs 3:5.
7. See Ephesians 6:18.
8. See Hebrews 4:12–16.
9. See Luke 16:13–14; Proverbs 29:25; James 1:14–15; Ephesians 2:3.
10. See James 3:17–18; Ephesians 4:25–5:2.
11. See 1 Corinthians 7:2–5; Proverbs 5:15–23; Song of Solomon.
12. See Ephesians 6:5–9.
13. See Luke 16:10–12; Romans 13:1–7; Matthew 22:21.
14. See 2 Peter 2:10.
15. See Romans 13:12–14; Galatians 5:16–21; 2 Timothy 2:22; 1 Corinthians 6.
16. See Martin Luther, "Defense and Explanation of All the Articles," 2nd article, in Collected Works.